McGREGOR ON DAMAGES

VOLUMES IN THE COMMON LAW LIBRARY

THE COMMON LAW LIBRARY

McGREGOR ON DAMAGES

SECOND SUPPLEMENT TO THE TWENTIETH EDITION

By

JAMES EDELMAN

A Justice of the High Court of Australia

SWEET & MAXWELL

THOMSON REUTERS

Published in 2019 by Thomson Reuters, trading as Sweet & Maxwell.
Registered in England & Wales. Company No. 1679046.
Registered office and address for service: 5 Canada Square, Canary Wharf,
London E14 5AQ.

For further information on our products and services, visit
http://www.sweetandmaxwell.co.uk.

Computerset by Sweet & Maxwell.
Printed and bound by CPI Group (UK) Ltd, Croydon, CR0 4YY.
No natural forests were destroyed to make this product; only farmed timber
was used and replanted.
A CIP catalogue record of this book is available from the British Library.

Main Work: 978-0-414-06415-7

Second Supplement: 978-0-414-07318-0

HOW TO USE THIS SUPPLEMENT

This is the Second Supplement to the Twentieth Edition of *McGregor on Damages*, and has been compiled according to the structure of the main volume.

At the beginning of each chapter of this Supplement, a mini table of contents of the sections in the main volume has been included. Where a heading in this table of contents has been marked with a square pointer, this indicates that there is relevant information in this Supplement to which the reader should refer. Material that is new to the Cumulative Supplement is indicated by the symbol ■. Material that has been included from the previous supplement is indicated by the symbol □.

Within each chapter, updating information is referenced to the relevant paragraph in the main volume.

TABLE OF CONTENTS

TABLE OF CASES

TABLE OF STATUTES

TABLE OF CIVIL PROCEDURE RULES AND RULES OF THE SUPREME COURT

INTRODUCTORY

1. A DEFINITION OF DAMAGES

(3) The omission of the reference to tort and breach of contract

(b) Damages in equity

(ii) Damages in equity's exclusive jurisdiction

After para.1-019, add a new paragraph:

An immediate qualification must be made. Just as an order for payment of a debt **1-019A** is not an award of damages, so too there are orders in equity made in claims that are akin to a claim for a debt and which are not properly conceived as damages. Those are claims for payment of a sum of money that would reconstitute a trust fund or that would require repayment of the value of misappropriated company property. In the House of Lords and Supreme Court decisions of *Target Holdings Ltd v Redferns* [1996] A.C. 421; [1995] 3 W.L.R. 352 and *AIB Group (UK) Plc v Mark Redler & Co* [2014] UKSC 58; [2015] A.C. 1503, the existence of such claims was doubted. But they have a long history in equity. Lower courts have generally applied strictly the approach taken in *Target* and *AIB* (see, for instance, *Wessely v White* [2018] EWHC 1499 (Ch); [2019] B.C.C. 289 at [45]–[46]), but in *Interactive Technology Corp Ltd v Ferster* [2018] EWCA Civ 1594; [2018] 2 P. & C.R. DG22 these decisions were brushed aside. The respondent director dishonestly withdrew more than £4 million from the appellant company in unauthorised remuneration. He argued that his services were worth the full value withdrawn. Orders were made for the calculation of compensation for losses. Before the Court of Appeal, the company sought to avoid any argument about causation of loss by arguing that only one species of equitable compensation, described as "reparative compensation", was concerned with compensation for losses. David Richards LJ (with whom Newey LJ agreed) accepted this submission, concluding that the other species, "substitutive compensation", which is akin to a claim for debt in equity, was not concerned with causation of loss but with "claims for a money payment as a substitute for performance of the trustee's obligation" (at [17]–[21]). Again, in *Main v Giambrone & Law (A Firm)* [2017] EWCA Civ 1193; [2018] P.N.L.R. 2, when solicitors released deposits paid by their clients, and held on trust, without fulfilling the requirement of receiving guarantees the solicitors were liable for equitable compensation, described as running in tandem with contractual damages for a "breach of contract [that] consisted of wrongfully paying out deposit monies which it had undertaken to keep safe" (at [63]).

PART 1A COMPENSATORY DAMAGES: OBJECT AND TERMINOLOGY

CHAPTER 2

THE OBJECT OF AN AWARD OF COMPENSATORY DAMAGES

TABLE OF CONTENTS

(1)   THE PRINCIPLE OF COMPENSATION

After para.2-001, add a new paragraph:

The meaning of "loss" is rarely defined. It encompasses any adverse conse-   **2-001A**
quences, both pecuniary and non-pecuniary. The assessment is undertaken at trial
with the benefit of hindsight. Hence, even the expenditure of money on a lavish
lifestyle that would not otherwise have been undertaken can be a recoverable loss
if the expenditure was caused by wrongdoing: *Barker v Winter* [2018] EWHC 1785
(QB).

CHAPTER 3

TERMINOLOGY USED IN COMPENSATORY DAMAGES AWARDS AND EXCLUSION CLAUSES

TABLE OF CONTENTS

(2)   NORMAL AND CONSEQUENTIAL LOSSES

In para.3-008, after the "various heads of damage.", add:

There is a very important distinction to be drawn between (i) an injury that car- **3-008**
ries with it a normal or usual loss, and (ii) the later consequential losses that are
actually suffered from the injury. These two types of damages are often described
as "normal" losses and "consequential" losses. They are, respectively, the usual or
generalised consequences of an injury and the actual consequences. The normal loss
is that loss which every claimant in a like situation will be expected to suffer; the
"particular" or "actual" consequential loss is that loss which is related to the
circumstances of the particular claimant. A rare example where the distinction was
highlighted in the context of personal injury was in *Brownlie v Four Seasons Holdings Inc* [2017] UKSC 80; [2018] 1 W.L.R. 192. Lord Sumption JSC (with whom
Lord Hughes JSC agreed), not in dissent on this point, explained that in a case of
personal injury, the damage to the claimant's bodily integrity is suffered as soon as
the bodily injury has occurred, "even if subsequent events are relevant to determine
the pecuniary measure of that damage": [2017] UKSC 80; [2018] 1 W.L.R. 192 at
[25]. The cause of action accrues at the time of the injury and limitation periods
begin to run from then. The damage that is immediately suffered and immediately
recoverable is that loss that is common to all claimants, usually described as "loss
of amenity".

**(b)   The division between normal measure and (particular) consequential
losses**

After para.3-016, add a new paragraph:

The converse principle should also apply where clauses provide for recovery of   **3-017**
"total loss". That reference to loss should be seen as a reference to both normal and
consequential losses rather than as an amelioration or abolition of rules such as
Hadley v Baxendale (1854) 9 Ex. 341; 156 E.R. 145. In *Lehman Brothers Finance
AG (In Liquidation) v Klaus Tschira Stiftung GmbH* [2019] EWHC 379 (Ch);
[2019] 2 All E.R. (Comm) 97 the issue concerned the extent of recovery of "total
losses and costs (or gain)" under an agreement. Snowden J held that a century and
a half after *Hadley v Baxendale* much clearer words needed to be used in order to
ensure total indemnity for all losses (at [213]). He said (at [208]–[210]) that this
result would follow whether one applied the remoteness test that restricted recovery
of damages due to reasons of policy as explained by Asquith LJ in *Victoria Laundry*

(Windsor) Ltd v Newman Industries Ltd [1949] 2 K.B. 528; [1949] 1 All E.R. 997 or, by the approach taken by Lord Hoffmann in *Transfield Shipping Inc v Mercator Shipping Inc (The Achilleas)* [2008] UKHL 48; [2009] 1 A.C. 61 at 69 [16], (see below at para.8-168 and following), because the law should not "impose on the [contracting party] a liability greater than he could reasonably have thought he was undertaking".

PART 1B THE HEADS OF COMPENSATORY DAMAGES

CHAPTER 5

NON-PECUNIARY LOSSES

II.   CONTRACT

(3)   MENTAL DISTRESS

After para.5-029, add a new paragraph:

5-029A   The present governing principle therefore requires focus upon the principal object of the contract rather than mere questions of foreseeability. But doubts have been expressed. "In such cases [namely, cases of ordinary commercial contracts]", Lord Millett (with whom Lord Bingham agreed) said in *Johnson v Unisys Ltd* [2001] UKHL 13; [2003] 1 A.C. 518 at [70] "non-pecuniary loss such as mental suffering consequent on breach is not within the contemplation of the parties and is accordingly too remote." But the rules in this area should not be seen as a special and unique application of remoteness of damage in contract and this statement should not be seen as a prescriptive rule. Lord Millett should not be taken to be saying anything more than that the lack of contemplation of the parties is generally sufficient to establish a lack of assumption of responsibility for the losses incurred. A focus upon the extent to which the object of the contract is to obtain psychological benefits is also the best way to assess whether there can reasonably be said to be an assumption of responsibility for the losses. More recently, cases have taken a nuanced approach, consistent with this overarching principle, by focusing upon the extent to which the object of the contract was concerned with psychological benefits. In *Shaw v Leigh Day (A Firm)* [2017] EWHC 825 (QB); [2017] P.N.L.R. 26, Andrews J held that a claim for distress should go to trial where it was arguable that the known objective of a legal retainer, to represent the claimant at an inquest into her father's death, was to obtain peace of mind (at [25], [29]). In contrast, in *Khan v University of Leeds* [2018] EWHC 912 (Ch), the claimant alleged a breach of the contract between her and the University by which it was conditionally agreed that she would be given a place to study for a PhD. The judge held that liability had not been proved, but, in obiter dicta, he considered the quantum of any non-pecuniary loss. The judge held that non-pecuniary loss would not have been awarded because it was "peripheral to the main educational purpose of her contract with the University" (at [81]).

PART 1C THE LIMITS OF COMPENSATORY DAMAGES

CHAPTER 7

REDUCTION OF DAMAGES FOR CONTRIBUTORY NEGLIGENCE

1. LIABILITY IN TORT

(2) Apportionment

After para.7-008, add a new paragraph:

Although an assessment of contributory negligence involves matters of impression, within a range of reasonable disagreement, there are basic principles of law to follow in the exercise of determining the extent of responsibility for damage. Three key points apply in the assessment of contributory negligence. First, the assessment is concerned with responsibility for, and hence contribution to, the damage suffered and not to the event that causes the damage. The classic example is the failure to wear a seatbelt which does not contribute to the event: *Assetco Plc v Grant Thornton UK LLP* [2019] EWHC 150 (Comm) at [1095]. Secondly, the claimant's contribution must be one cause of that damage: (at [1096]). Hence, fault that makes no causal contribution to damage cannot be taken into account no matter how blameworthy the claimant (at [1097] citing the 20th edition of this work at para.7-009). Thirdly, the extent of the causal potency, and not merely the blameworthiness, will affect the reduction (at [1097]).

7-008A

After para.7-009, add a new paragraph:

An assessment of a claimant's relative blameworthiness will be based upon all circumstances but a key factor will be the extent to which the claimant could have foreseen her or his loss. This foreseeability will, in turn, be affected by the extent to which the claimant has been "reasonably induced to believe that he may proceed with safety" (*Assetco Plc v Grant Thornton UK LLP* [2019] EWHC 150 (Comm) at [1098]–[1099]) and particularly where he or she has been so induced by the defendant.

7-009A

After para.7-010, add new paragraphs:

Another difficult issue is how to assess the causal potency of the contribution by a company in an action against a negligent auditor for losses arising from a failure to detect the company's wrongdoing. In some jurisdictions it has been held that for the purposes of contributory negligence, where the very duty of the auditors is to detect company wrongdoing, there should be no reduction in the award of dam-

7-010A

ages for contributory negligence based on the company's wrongdoing: *Livent Inc v Deloitte LLP* [2016] ONCA 11 at [103]; *AWA Ltd v Daniels* (1992) 7 ACSR 759 at 842. However, accepting that auditors should bear some responsibility for the event about which the "very reason" for their duty was to prevent, as in *Reeves v Commissioner of Police of the Metropolis* [2000] 1 A.C. 360; [1999] 3 W.L.R. 363, does not require one to accept that the auditors were entirely responsible for all the damage. Hence, in Reeves there was a reduction of 50% in the liability of the police due to the prisoner's responsibility for his suicide. Similarly, as Bryan J observed in *Assetco Plc v Grant Thornton UK LLP* [2019] EWHC 150 (Comm) at [1105], there is a reduction of causation potency, and hence responsibility, of auditors for a company's own wrongdoing: *Barings v Coopers and Lybrand (No.7)* [2003] EWHC 1319 (Ch); [2003] Lloyd's Rep I.R. 566 at [698]–[720] and *Singularis Holdings Ltd v Daiwa Capital Markets Europe Ltd* [2018] EWCA Civ 84; [2018] 1 W.L.R. 2777 at [94].

7-010B   In *Assetco Plc v Grant Thornton UK LLP* [2019] EWHC 150 (Comm) at [1185], Bryan J concluded that notwithstanding the fraud of the directors, the negligence of the accountants was "flagrant", being of the "utmost gravity", "just short of recklessness" and going to the "very heart of an auditor's duties". Apportionment was properly assessed separately in relation to each of the events of damage. A 25% reduction was made for both wasted expenditure and a fraudulent related party payment of £1.5 million (see *Assetco Plc v Grant Thornton UK LLP* [2019] EWHC 191 (Comm) at [14], [21]).

CHAPTER 8

REMOTENESS OF DAMAGE

TABLE OF CONTENTS

I. TORT

(A) CAUSATION

2. CAUSE IN FACT: THE NORM AND THE EXCEPTIONS

(1) The norm

Replace footnote 38 with:

8-015 [38] See also *Darnley v Croydon Health Services NHS Trust* [2018] UKSC 50; [2019] A.C. 831.

(2) The exceptions

(a) Negligence

At the end of the third paragraph in para.8-023, after "material contribution to the outcome.", add:

8-023 A "material difference" to the outcome, as applied in later cases (see, for instance, *NAX v King's College Hospital NHS Foundation Trust* [2018] EWHC 1170 (QB); [2018] Med. L.R. 431 at [120] and Annex [4]) must mean either (i) an outcome which involves a lesser injury, in which case the loss is assessed by reference to the worsened injury that could have been avoided, or (ii) no injury at all, in which case the loss is assessed by reference to the entire injury.

After para.8-029, add a new paragraph:

8-029A *Chester* was narrowly confined in *Duce v Worcestershire Acute Hospitals NHS Trust* [2018] EWCA Civ 1307; [2018] P.I.Q.R. P18. There, an operation was performed on the claimant without negligence. However, she suffered nerve damage about which she had not been warned. Hamblen LJ (with whom Newey LJ agreed) applied the approach taken in *Correia v University Hospital of North Staffordshire NHS Trust* [2017] EWCA Civ 356; [2017] E.C.C. 37 at [28] that the exceptional principle of causation in *Chester* requires a claimant to plead and prove that, if warned of the risk, the claimant would have deferred the operation (at [70]). Leggatt LJ reached the same conclusion but further confined *Chester* to the situation where the claimant would not have had the operation at all (at [84]). However, he considered that once a claimant proved that he or she would not have had the operation at that time, the onus of proving that the claimant would not have had the operation at all would then shift to the wrongdoing defendant (at [91]). Chester must also be confined to recovery only for the losses flowing from those duties about which there was a failure to warn. Hence, in *Khan v Meadows* [2019] EWCA Civ 152; [2019] 4 W.L.R 26, a doctor who negligently failed to warn about a risk that a child would be born with haemophilia was liable only for the additional costs of upbringing due to the haemophilia but not the unrelated costs of the child's condition of autism.

4.   CAUSE IN LAW: CONSEQUENCES FOLLOWING UPON A NEW INTERVENING FORCE

At the end of para.8-036, after "for his conduct.", add:
But, when contributory negligence and mitigation are put aside, an intervening act by a claimant involves the same considerations of remoteness as intervening acts of third parties: *Clay v TUI UK Ltd* [2018] EWCA Civ 1177; [2018] 4 All E.R. 672.   **8-036**

(2)   Intervening acts of the claimant

(a)   Acts where the claimant is not a completely free chooser

(iv)   Acts by claimants when subject to a disability imposed by the tort

Replace the paragraph with:
Where physical injury caused by the defendant's wrongful act limits the   **8-074**
claimant's facility of movement and action, the defendant may be liable for further injury arising from this lack of facility. In *Wieland v Cyril Lord Carpets*,[377] the claimant, soon after leaving the hospital where she had had a collar fitted to her neck which had been injured two days previously in an accident due to the defendants' negligence, fell as she was descending some stairs with her son, thereby sustaining injury to her ankles. Apart from being in a rather nervous condition at the time due to a combination of her visit to the doctor and the shake-up from the accident, the constriction of the movement of her head caused by the collar deprived the claimant of her usual ability to adjust herself automatically to the bifocal glasses which she had worn for many years, and these factors together produced some unsteadiness. Eveleigh J held the claimant entitled to recover for the injury to her ankles because he regarded this further injury as attributable to the original negligence of the defendants. Not only, he said, has it

"long been recognised that injury sustained in one accident may be the cause of a subsequent injury"[378]

but also

"it can be said that it is foreseeable that one injury may affect a person's ability to cope with the vicissitudes of life and thereby be a cause of another injury".[379]

With this case should be contrasted *McKew v Holland and Hannen and Cubitts*,[380] where the House of Lords held against the claimant in his claim in respect of a further and severe injury caused by falling down a staircase when his left leg unexpectedly gave way beneath him, which it had a tendency to do on occasions as a result of a minor injury for which the defendants were admittedly liable. The circumstances giving rise to the fall were, however, markedly different from those in the earlier case, occurring nearly a month after the original accident when the claimant, holding his child by the hand, made to descend a steep staircase without a handrail and without the available assistance of his wife and brother-in-law. This act was sufficiently unreasonable to break the chain of causation so that the further injury fell to be regarded as caused by the claimant's own conduct. Lord Reid, with whom Lords Hodson and Dilhorne expressly concurred,[381] thought that this result followed even if the claimant's conduct was foreseeable. He said:

> "It is often easy to foresee unreasonable conduct or some other novus actus interveniens as being quite likely. But that does not mean that the defender must pay for damage caused by the novus actus. It only leads to trouble that if one tries to graft on to the concept of foreseeability some rule of law to the effect that a wrongdoer is not bound to foresee something which in fact he could readily foresee as quite likely to happen. For it is not at all unlikely or unforeseeable that an active man who has suffered such a disability will take some quite unreasonable risk. But if he does he cannot hold the defender liable for the consequences."[382]

Here then the defendant is taken not to have caused an injury which was foreseeable, and, while this result is a perfectly proper one in exceptional cases,[383] it would be unwise to reach too readily the conclusion that a defendant ceases to be liable for foreseeable consequences merely because they have arisen out of unreasonable conduct on the part of the claimant. It might even be asked whether it would not have been better for the House to have held the defendant liable but to have made a very substantial reduction from the claimant's damages on account of his contributory negligence, thereby adopting the approach taken practically contemporaneously, in the context of a ship collision, by Brandon J in *The Calliope*.[384] However, a similar approach was applied in *Clay v TUI UK Ltd* [2018] EWCA Civ 1177; [2018] 4 All E.R. 672. In that case, a defective locking mechanism in a hotel sliding door caused the claimant and his family to be locked on a balcony. The claimant fractured his skull when, after trying to attract attention for 30 minutes, he climbed over the balustrade of the balcony in order to step onto the next balcony. The trial judge, and a majority of the Court of Appeal (Hamblen and Kitchin LJJ) held that despite the inconvenience to his family in waiting longer, when no help might have been found, the claimant's act was "so unexpected and/or foolhardy as to be a novus actus interveniens" (at [20], [46], [107]). A neater approach, and closer to that advocated above, was taken in *Darnley v Croydon Health Services NHS Trust* [2018] UKSC 50; [2019] A.C. 831, where the Supreme Court held that it was reasonably foreseeable that a claimant would leave the accident and emergency department of a hospital with a serious head injury after 19 minutes when the claimant had been told that he would have to wait for four or five hours. No enquiry was made about the reasonableness of the claimant's conduct.

[377] [1969] 3 All E.R. 1006.

[378] [1969] 3 All E.R. 1006 at 1009.

[379] [1969] 3 All E.R. 1006 at 1010.

[380] [1969] 3 All E.R. 1621 HL; 1970 S.C. (H.L.) 20.

[381] Lord Upjohn merely concurred; Lord Guest, in a separate speech, took the view that the claimant had behaved unreasonably in attempting to save himself by leaping forward down the stairs, and therefore had two reasons for holding against him: [1969] 3 All E.R. 1621 HL at 1625 to 1626.

[382] [1969] 3 All E.R. 1621 HL at 1623.

[383] See para.8-035, above.

[384] [1970] P. 172; [1970] 2 W.L.R. 991 at para.6-015, above. See too *Environment Agency v Ellis* [2008] EWCA Civ 1117; [2009] P.I.Q.R. P5 CA at 85 in the footnote at the end of para.6-014, above; facts at para.10-018, below.

(B) SCOPE OF PROTECTION: THE LIMITS OF POLICY

2. FORESEEABLE DAMAGE CAUSED IN AN UNFORESEEABLE MANNER OR TO AN UNFORESEEABLE DEGREE WHERE A BREACH OF A DUTY TO THE CLAIMANT TO TAKE CARE HAS BEEN ESTABLISHED

(1) Direct consequences

(b) Existing states of affairs: pecuniary abnormalities of the claimant or of his property

(ii) Weakness

After para.8-113, add a new paragraph:

It is necessary to reiterate that the loss arising from impecuniosity must still be reasonably foreseeable even if the precise sequence by which that loss is caused need not be. In *Nautical Challenge Ltd v Evergreen Marine (UK) Ltd* [2019] EWHC 163 (Admlty); [2019] 1 Lloyd's Rep. 543 the claim arose as a result of a maritime collision between the parties' respective ships, the *Alexandra 1* and the ironically named *Ever Smart*. The liability for the collision was apportioned 20:80. Nautical Challenge, who bore 20% responsibility, was impecunious and suffered further loss due to its inability to pay for its collision repairs in cash. Evergreen Marine submitted that it could only be liable for this impecuniosity under *Lagden v O'Connor* if the impecuniosity was reasonably foreseeable. It submitted that the passage at para.8-113 of the 20th edition of this work had incorrectly suggested that reasonable foreseeability was unnecessary. Andrew Baker J quite correctly, and efficiently, disposed of this submission saying that the point was "only that so long as relevant impecuniosity is foreseeable there is no call for an enquiry into precisely how or why the particular claimant came to be materially impecunious" (at [52]–[53]). In other words, it is not the "circumstances of a particular case" that must reasonably be foreseen. In any event, however, the claim for this head of loss failed because it was perfectly obvious to Nautical Challenge that it was not going to receive a prompt payout from its underwriters and, acting reasonably, it should not have delayed in acting promptly to obtain the credit for the repairs that it ultimately did obtain. **8-113A**

4. DAMAGE OUTSIDE THE SCOPE OF THE DUTY

Replace para.8-135 with:

Some cases, indeed most cases, are easy. Thus in *Darby v National Trust*,[702] where the duty to warn against swimming in a pond was directed to the danger of catching Weil's disease, there could be no liability for death by drowning as this fell outside the scope of the duty to warn against swimming.[703] Also reasonably straightforward is Lord Hoffmann's "over-simplified"[704] illustration in *SAAMCO*,[705] now cited, it seems, upon every conceivable occasion, of the man who would not **8-135** have gone mountaineering had he been properly advised by his doctor of a weak knee.[706] It is not going to be part of the duty of the doctor to protect the man from accidents unrelated to the condition of his knee. If, on the other hand, the accident, or any other accident, is attributable to the knee and happens in the course of an activity in which the man would not have engaged but for the doctor's advice, this would fall within the scope of the duty. But cases can be difficult to resolve as to the scope of the duty, as is shown by the opposing views often taken of a case by the House of Lords, the Court of Appeal and the court of first instance. Contrasts abound. Thus whereas in *SAAMCO* the valuers were held liable only for the loss resulting from the over-valuation and not for the much greater loss from the property market collapse, in *Aneco Reinsurance Underwriting v Johnson & Higgins*,[707] where brokers had failed to effect valid insurance, they were held liable not just for the loss resulting from their failure properly to insure but for the much greater loss resulting from their client having no reinsurance at all. In *Khan v Meadows* [2019] EWCA Civ 152; [2019] 4 W.L.R 26, a further twist concerning scope of duty involved whether the additional costs of the birth of a child with autism fell within a doctor's scope of a duty to warn about the risk that a child would be born with haemophilia. The Court of Appeal (Nicola Davies LJ giving the judgment) held that they did not fall within the scope of that duty. The purpose of the consultation with the doctor was to give advice about whether a future child would carry the haemophilia gene (at [27]). The risk of a child being born with autism was not increased by the advice given by the doctor (at [28]). Indeed, the respondent would have accepted the risk of a child being born with autism (at [26]).

[702] [2001] EWCA Civ 189; [2001] P.I.Q.R. P27 CA at 372.

[703] See [2001] EWCA Civ 189; [2001] P.I.Q.R. P27 CA at 377–378.

[704] *BPE Solicitors v Hughes-Holland* [2017] UKSC 21; [2018] A.C. 599 at [1].

[705] [1997] A.C. 191; [1996] 3 W.L.R. 87.

[706] [1997] A.C. 191 at 213D.

[707] [2001] UKHL 51; [2002] 1 Lloyd's Rep. 157 HL.

After para.8-135, add new paragraphs:

8-135A   As Lord Sumption explained in in *BPE Solicitors v Hughes-Holland* [2017] UKSC 21; [2018] A.C. 599, the extent to which an assumption of responsibility will concern the risks of a transaction will depend upon whether the transaction is one of "advice", involving the underlying concept of an adviser who guides the "whole decision making process" including entry into the transaction and is responsible for the consequences of entry ([at 40]), or "information" involving the concept of a general information provider who does not take responsibility for the decision to enter the transaction ([at 41]). However, it is not the descriptively inadequate ([at 39]) labels of "advice" or "information" that are important but the underlying concepts.

8-135B   Every case will turn upon its own circumstances when ascertaining whether the transaction was one by which the defendant assumed responsibility for the whole transaction or only for the correctness of the advice. Two contrasting examples can be given. In *Manchester Building Society v Grant Thornton UK LLP* [2019] EWCA Civ 40; [2019] 1 W.L.R. 4610, the respondent accountants were negligent in their accounting treatment of long-term interest rate swaps entered by the building society. The swaps were closed after the error was discovered, with £32.5 million in break costs. The building society would not have entered those swaps if it had known of the error in the accounting treatment but its decision to enter the swaps was based upon a number of commercial considerations upon which the accountants were not asked to advise. Hamblen LJ, with whom Males LJ and Dame Elizabeth Gloster agreed, held that the accountants had not been involved with, and had not assumed responsibility, for the building society's decision to enter the swap (at [63]–[64]). The loss suffered by closing out the swaps, at market value, on discovery of the error was a loss on the transaction as a whole. The error did not compel the building society to incur a loss by closing out the swaps at an earlier time than would otherwise have avoided the loss ([at 89]). In contrast, in *Main v Giambrone* [2017] EWCA Civ 1193; [2018] P.N.L.R. 2, a law firm advised English and Irish claimants that they would be protected by bank loan guarantees when buying Italian property off the plan. The firm received and then paid out the claimant's deposits without guarantees being in place. The firm, with its Italian lawyers, were found to have guided the "whole decision making process" and therefore to have assumed responsibility for the whole transaction which turned out to be a money laundering scam (at [82]). It was therefore liable for the deposits lost by the claimants.

II. CONTRACT

(A) CAUSATION

Replace para.8-141 with:

One significant issue of causation that arises in relation to damages for breach   **8-141**
of contract concerns whether damages can be claimed for the loss of a bargain following termination for a breach that is not repudiatory. Damages for lost profits following termination can only be recovered where the termination arises due to a repudiatory breach: *Financings Ltd v Baldock* [1963] 2 Q.B. 104 CA; [1963] 2 W.L.R. 359. The reason for this is that the general law's recognition that a breach is sufficient for termination means that when termination occurs the breach has caused the loss of the bargain. But if the right to terminate arises only by some contractual provision, the trigger of which might be described as a breach or might not, then it is the innocent party's reliance upon the contractual provision, not the breach, that causes the loss of the bargain. However, difficult questions can arise where a claimant terminates the contract in reliance upon a contractual term but where an independent ground for termination existed at general law. As Andrew Baker J said in *Phones 4u Ltd (In Administration) v EE Ltd* [2018] EWHC 49 (Comm); [2018] 2 All E.R. (Comm) 315, a claim for loss of bargain damages for losses arising from termination for a repudiatory breach required a causal link between the termination and the repudiatory breach (at [122]). In *Phones 4u Ltd*, summary judgment was granted against the defendant's counterclaim for loss of bargain damages because the reason given by the defendant for terminating was the appointment of an administrator. The defendant did not rely, when terminating, upon the inability of the claimant to perform the contract. As the judge noted, the basic principle gives rise to a number of difficult questions if (i) no reason is given for termination, or (ii) the reason given is a contractual right based on circumstances that also amount to repudiatory breach. The answers to these issues should be (i) the reason must be discerned from the objective circumstances, and (ii) the reason is construed closely to determine whether it relies both upon the contractual right, simpliciter, and the repudiatory circumstances that gave rise to the right (see at [125]–[127]).

(B) SCOPE OF PROTECTION: CONTEMPLATION OF THE PARTIES

4. THE IMPACT OF THE DECISION IN THE ACHILLEAS IN 2008

(2) The aftermath of the decision

After para.8-178, add a new paragraph:

8-178A Both the assumption of responsibility approach and the traditional approach were applied by Jay J in *ARB v IVF Hammersmith Ltd* [2017] EWHC 2438 (QB); [2018] 2 W.L.R. 1223, where substantial damages were refused as a matter of policy (see below at para.40-293A) for an IVF clinic's breach of its contractual duty of care in implanting frozen embryos without the consent of the father (which purported consent had been forged by the mother). The trial judge, Jay J, held that if the damages had been recoverable then they would not have been too remote. Applying both the assumption of responsibility and the traditional approaches (at [331]) he concluded that the losses were of the same type as those for which the clinic had assumed responsibility and that it was irrelevant that the forgery was outside the contemplation of the parties because the duty was one to take reasonable care to avoid an outcome; that outcome occurred and the losses flowed naturally from it and were not unusual (at [334]). There was no market understanding or expectation that these damages would be irrecoverable (at [337]). An appeal to the Court of Appeal based on liability was dismissed, so the Court of Appeal did not need to consider further these questions of remoteness of damages (*ARB v IVF Hammersmith* [2018] EWCA Civ 2803; [2019] 2 W.L.R. 1094 at [35], [61]).

After para.8-181, add a new sub-section and paragraph:

(3) Assumption of Responsibility and Causation

8-181A Assumption of responsibility is a part of the doctrine of remoteness of damages. It is quite separate from the rules of causation. This point was underscored by the decision of the Supreme Court in *Tiuta International Ltd v De Villiers Surveyors Ltd* [2017] UKSC 77; [2017] 1 W.L.R. 4627. In *Tiuta International Ltd*, a valuer was assumed to have been negligent for the purposes of a summary judgment application and the issue was whether the valuer was liable to the lender for the loss of the full value of the loan of around £3.1 million when the borrower defaulted. £2.8 million of the loan was given to refinance an earlier loan by the lender and the lender had not alleged negligence by the valuer in relation to the first loan. Hence, the valuer argued, it had not caused £2.8 million of the lender's loss which would have been lost in any event. In contrast, the lender argued that although the £2.8 million would have been lost under the first loan, the valuer had contemplated that he might be liable for that amount if he were negligent in valuing the property for the second loan and so, the lender argued, the valuer should be liable for the full amount. The Supreme Court, overturning the Court of Appeal, rejected this argument and upheld the valuer's claim for summary judgment in relation to the £2.8 million. The assumption of responsibility of the valuer might have been relevant to remoteness issues but it was not relevant to the basic question of causation (at [10]). Without causation there is no issue of remoteness of damage.

CHAPTER 9

MITIGATION OF DAMAGE

TABLE OF CONTENTS

I.   Various Meanings of the Term "Mitigation"

1.   Principal Meaning: The Three Rules as to the Avoiding of the Consequences of a Wrong

Replace para.9-007 with:

9-007   These three rules were endorsed in *Thai Airways International Public Co Ltd v KI Holdings Co Ltd.*[2] In that case, Thai Airways claimed damages from KI Holdings for breaches of contract in relation to the supply of economy class aircraft seats. Some seats were delivered late and others were not delivered. Thai Airways was prevented from using five of its aircraft for 18 months pending the delivery of the seats from another supplier. The issue at trial was whether Thai Airways had mitigated its loss. Leggatt J endorsed these three different rules for mitigation,[3] although suggesting that the three rules had an underlying unity based on causation. There is some underlying unity in the notion of "factual" causation but "factual" causation is not sufficient. As Leggatt J recognised[4] the unity also lies in a rule that damages are assessed as if the claimant acted reasonably, if in fact it did not act reasonably. The discussion in this chapter is consistent with the concept of acting reasonably as deconstructed into various norms including the dominant norm that it is reasonable for a claimant to enter an available market as soon as possible to obtain a substitute for a defendant's performance.

[2] [2015] EWHC 1250 (Comm); [2016] 1 All E.R. (Comm) 675. And again in *Assetco Plc v Grant Thornton UK LLP* [2019] EWHC 150 (Comm) at [882].

[3] [2015] EWHC 1250 (Comm); [2016] 1 All E.R. (Comm) 675 at [32].

[4] [2015] EWHC 1250 (Comm); [2016] 1 All E.R. (Comm) 675 at [33], quoting Dyson and Kramer (2014) 130 L.Q.R. 259 at 263. See also *Assetco Plc v Grant Thornton UK LLP* [2019] EWHC 150 (Comm) at [884].

II.   The Rule as to Avoidable Loss: No Recovery for Loss Which the Claimant Ought Reasonably to have Avoided

1.   Various Aspects of the Rule

(a)   Application to contract and tort

At the end of para.9-015, after "mutandis, to tort.", add:

9-015   In cases of both breach of contract and tort the mitigation principle concerns whether losses "flow" from a past cause, based upon whether the claimant acted reasonably: *Dhaliwal v Hussain* [2017] EWHC 2655 (Ch) at [149].

4.   Standard of Conduct which the Claimant must Attain when Assessing what Steps should have been Taken by Him

(1)   The criterion of reasonableness and the standard of reasonableness

To the end of the first sentence, after "an admitted wrongdoer.", add new footnote 307a:

9-079   [307a] See also *Rabilizirov v A2 Dominion London Ltd* [2019] EWHC 186 (QB); [2019] T.C.L.R. 4 at [76].

IV. The Rule as to Avoided Loss: No Recovery Generally for Loss Which the Claimant has Avoided by Reasonably Necessary Means

1. The Three Subdivisions of the Rule

At the end of para.9-112, replace "test is again not causation." with:

limited role for causation is that a lack of "factual" causation will negate mitiga- **9-112** tion where the event that gives rise to the benefit would have occurred in any event despite the wrongdoing. So too, "legal causation", or remoteness, requires that the connection between the wrong and the action leading to the benefit not be too remote. An example is the decision in *Assetco Plc v Grant Thornton UK LLP* [2019] EWHC 150 (Comm), where one sufficient reason for rejecting the defendant's submission that the claimant had mitigated its loss was that a scheme of arrange- ment would have taken place despite the negligence of the auditors. Another suf- ficient reason was that the scheme was said to be too remote from, or not the "legal cause of" the auditors' negligence, resulting instead from the creditors' decision in relation to the company's perilous financial position: [2019] EWHC 150 (Comm) at [897].

4. Actions Taken After the Wrong by Third Parties

After para.9-155, add a new paragraph:

Lowick Rose LLP v Swynson Ltd contrasts with the decision of the Supreme **9-155A** Court in *Tiuta International Ltd v De Villiers Surveyors Ltd* [2017] UKSC 77; [2017] 1 W.L.R. 4627, where the alleged benefit to the claimant was neither col- lateral nor reduced the loss. In *Tiuta International Ltd v De Villiers Surveyors Ltd*, the facts assumed for the summary judgment application were that the claimant made a loan of around £2.5 million for a development, secured by a charge over the development. It did so after the respondent had valued the development at £2.3 million in its then current state and £4.5 million at completion. Later, a second loan of around £3.1 million was made, again secured by a charge over the develop- ment, with £2.8 million to refinance the debt from the first loan. After the debtor went into administration without repaying any of the second loan, the lender claimed damages from the valuer for negligence in its valuation of the second loan only. The valuer sought summary judgment in the amount of £2.8 million which, it said, would have been owing under the first loan, and therefore lost, in any event. The Supreme Court held that the court could not disregard, as a collateral benefit, the action taken by the borrower to discharge the first loan for two reasons: it was not a benefit and it was not collateral. First, the discharge of the existing debt did not confer a benefit on the lender because the second loan, from which the discharge was made, increased the exposure of the lender to the same extent. Secondly, the discharge was not collateral because it was required by the very terms of the second loan. The substance of the second loan was really just an additional loan of about £300,000 (at [13]). The whole litigation was conducted on the premise that the valuer had not been negligent in the valuation for the first loan. As the Supreme Court recognised, if he had been negligent then although that first loan was discharged, it would be at least arguable that his negligence in relation to the second loan was not confined to a loss of £300,000 but extended also to the loss of the value of the lender's claim under the, now repaid, first loan (at [13]). This way, a valuer cannot escape the consequences of his negligence by an act of further negligence.

5. ACTIONS TAKEN BEFORE THE WRONG BY THE CLAIMANT

(2) Sub-contracts already made before breach

(a) Sale

(ii) The position today

Replace para.9-183 with:

9-183   In summary, it is suggested that, in this uncertain and fluid state of the authorities in this small but important corner of the mitigation issue, the best solution may be this. Whatever the breach, whether it be by non-delivery, delayed delivery or defective delivery, the presumption should be that the buyer is entitled to have his sub-sale ignored but the seller is also entitled to rebut this presumption if he can show positively that the buyer neither has bought substitute goods after the breach nor is subject to a damages claim from his sub-buyer. And this solution should apply equally, mutatis mutandis, to contracts of carriage of goods. It is a solution that is in accordance with the rule that the burden of proof on the issue of mitigation is on the party in breach.[688] This solution was neatly applied in *Euro-Asian Oil SA v Credit Suisse AG* [2018] EWCA Civ 1720; [2019] 1 All E.R. (Comm) 706 , where *Agius* was gently set aside and the loss limited to the loss on the sub-sale because the cargo of oil that was not delivered was known by the parties to be nominated to perform a sub-contract; there was no possibility that the cargo would be put to any other use.

[688] On the onus of proof for avoided loss see para.9-115, above.

CHAPTER 10

CERTAINTY OF DAMAGE AND LOSS OF CHANCE

TABLE OF CONTENTS

I. THE PROBLEM OF CERTAINTY

Replace all three paragraphs in para.10-006 with:

Further cases presenting this difficulty of showing the amount of profitable sales **10-006**
that would have been made by the claimant had there been no tort or breach of
contract by the defendant have indicated that the claimant is assisted by the principle
in the very old case of *Armory v Delamirie* (1722) 1 Str. 505, which has today
received a new lease of life, the principle being that the court is required to resolve
uncertainties by making assumptions generous to the claimant where it is the
defendant's wrongdoing which has created those uncertainties. That principle was
endorsed by the Supreme Court in *One Step (Support) Ltd v Morris-Garner* [2018]
UKSC 20; [2019] A.C. 649 at [38] but there remains doubt about the extent of its
application. The doubt concerns whether the principle is one of general application or whether it applies only to assist the judge in resolving evidential disputes.
The remarks of Lord Reed JSC in *Morris-Garner* suggest the latter. So too, do the
remarks of Longmore LJ (with whom Arden and Aikens LJJ agreed) in *Keefe v The
Isle of Man Steam Packet Co Ltd* [2010] EWCA Civ 683 at [19], adopted in *Fluor
v Shanghai Zhenhua Heavy Industry Co Ltd* [2018] EWHC 1 (TCC); 178 Con. L.R.

210 at [53], that when the defendant's breach of duty makes it difficult or impossible for a claimant to adduce relevant evidence the defendant "must run the risk of adverse factual findings."

The basis of the principle as one that resolves evidential disputes can be seen in the refusal of Hamblen J to apply the *Armory v Delamirie* principle to the facts in *Porton Capital Technology Funds v 3M UK Holdings Ltd* [2011] EWHC 2895 (Comm). In 2007 the defendants in *Porton* agreed to buy the entire shareholding of a company from the shareholder claimants. The consideration for the purchase was a cash sum together with what was referred to as an earn out payment based on net sales for the year 2009, the defendants being required to continue the business. The earn out payment was the principal return to be made by the claimants from the sale. The defendants in breach of contract closed down the business so that there were no sales in 2009. The claimants, relying on *Armory v Delamirie*, argued that, since the very actions of the defendants in breaching the contract had made the quantification of damages more difficult, the court should resolve any uncertainties in the claimants' favour. Hamblen J did not accept the argument. The claim was for lost profits for breach of contract where there was evidence and documentation relating to the claim; the evidential playing field was a level one. *The Armory v Delamirie* principle should not be extended further than its evidentiary basis permits (at [244]).

To the extent that cases such as *Fearns v Anglo-Dutch Paint & Chemical Co Ltd* [2010] EWHC 1708 (Ch) at [70] and *Double Communications Ltd v News Corp International Ltd* [2011] EWHC 961 (QB) at [4] and [5] could be read as taking a broader approach, that approach should not be accepted. On one view, the *Armory v Delamirie* principle was also expanded by the Court of Appeal in *Gulati v MGN Ltd* [2015] EWCA Civ 1291; [2017] Q.B. 149 at [107], where the Court of Appeal upheld sizeable awards for phone hacking despite the absence in some cases of any records detailing the hacking and other wrongful activities. In the judgment with which the other judges agreed, Arden LJ said that the award of damages was

"an example of the ability of the law to prevent a person responsible for wrongdoing from escaping liability to his victim, without disturbing the general rule as to the conditions of liability."

On an expansive view, Arden LJ might be read as suggesting that a claim can be brought for loss caused by hacking against a proved hacker without proving any of the instances of hacking. This cannot be what Arden LJ meant. Her Ladyship's remarks are better understood as suggesting that in all of the circumstances of that case, inferences can be drawn of the nature and extent of the hacking which occurred based on the extent of the related wrongdoing by MGN.

II CIRCUMSTANCES IN WHICH DAMAGES MAY BE AWARDED ALTHOUGH THE NATURE OF THE DAMAGE PREVENTS ABSOLUTE CERTAINTY OF PROOF

5. WHERE IT IS UNCERTAIN WHETHER A PARTICULAR PECUNIARY LOSS WILL BE OR WOULD HAVE BEEN INCURRED

(4) Loss of a chance

(b) The range of the loss of a chance doctrine: general principles

(ii) The distinction between causation of loss and quantification of loss

Replace para.10-047 with:

It is submitted that losses of a chance appearing in the process of quantification **10-047** do not fall within the loss of a chance doctrine. Loss of a chance proper, as it may be termed, has a more limited field. It comes in before we get to quantification; indeed it comes in at the causation stage. How is this? It is because there are situations where the law has recognised, and has treated, the loss of a chance as a form of loss, an identifiable head of loss in itself. To take Lord Hoffmann's way of putting it in *Barker v Corus (UK) Ltd*,[184]

> "the law treats the loss of a chance of a favourable outcome as compensatable damage in itself".[185]

Causation is then established by showing that the claimant has lost the chance and showing this on the balance of probabilities. This then makes for three stages in the enquiry: first, it must be ascertained whether loss of a chance is recognised as a head of damage or loss in itself; secondly, it must be shown that on the balance of probabilities the claimant has lost the particular chance; thirdly, the lost chance must be quantified by resort to percentages and proportions.[186] The estimate of a lost chance at the third stage does not involve a balance of probabilities calculation of the precise chance but instead involves estimates of the loss by making the best attempt on the evidence to evaluate the value of the chances lost: *Parabola Investments Ltd v Browallia Cal Ltd* [2010] EWCA Civ 486; [2011] Q.B. 477 at [23], and see, most recently, *Rocker v Full Circle Asset Management* [2017] EWHC 2999 (QB) at [295]; *UBS AG (London Branch) v Kommunale Wasserwerke Leipzig GmbH* [2017] EWCA Civ 1567; [2017] 2 Lloyd's Rep. 621 at [284]. This is a broad brush evaluative exercise with which appellate courts are reluctant to interfere: *Wellesley Partners LLP v Withers LLP* [2015] EWCA Civ 1146; [2016] Ch. 529 CA at [125]; *UBS AG (London Branch) v Kommunale Wasserwerke Leipzig GmbH* [2017] EWCA Civ 1567; [2017] 2 Lloyd's Rep. 621 at [285]. As Marcus Smith J said in *Britned Development v ABB AB* [2018] EWHC 2616 (Ch); [2019] Bus. L.R. 718 at [12(6)], after quoting from this paragraph in the 20th edition, the quantification of damages does not proceed on the balance of probabilities but instead takes into account "all manner of risks and possibilities" in what Popplewell J described in *Asda Stores Ltd v Mastercard Inc* [2017] EWHC 93 (Comm); [2017] U.K.C.L.R. 283 at [306] as a "pragmatic approach".

[184] [2006] UKHL 20; [2006] 2 A.C. 572. This difficult case is considered at paras 10-021 and 10-022, above and para.10-056, below

[185] [2006] UKHL 20; [2006] 2 A.C. 572 at [36].

[186] What Toulson LJ convincingly says at [23] of his judgment in *Parabola Investments Ltd v Browallia Cal Ltd* [2010] EWCA Civ 486; [2011] Q.B. 477. (facts at para.10-037, above) and what Patten LJ equally convincingly says at [25] of his judgment in *Vasiliou v Hajigeorgiou* [2010] EWCA Civ 1475 (facts at para.10-038, above) fully support the analysis set out here. The term "loss of a chance proper" is there used; while Patten LJ has "loss of chance as such". See too, in *AerCap Partners Ltd v Avia Asset Management AB* [2010] EWHC 2431 (Comm); [2011] Bus. L.R. D85, Gross LJ's exploration of the distinction between all or nothing causation and percentage loss of a chance in relation to an issue where there was no hope of loss of a chance applying: [2010] EWHC 2431 (Comm); [2011] Bus. L.R. D85 at [70]–[77], especially the detailed [76].

Replace para.10-048 with:

10-048   The circumstances in which the law is prepared to recognise the loss of a chance as itself an identifiable head of loss, and as itself constituting compensable damage, are when the provision of the chance is the object of the duty that has been breached. This comes out clearly in *Chaplin v Hicks* itself where Fletcher Moulton LJ emphasised that

> "the very object and scope of the contract were to give the plaintiff the chance of being selected a prize-winner".[187]

Finally, in *Britned Development v ABB AB* [2018] EWHC 2616 (Ch); [2019] Bus. L.R. 718 at [427], it was held that the object and scope of a statutory duty to protect competition from attempts to undermine it did not require proof of actual loss; loss of a chance was within the scope of the provision: Treaty on the Functioning of the European Union art.101.

[187] [1911] 2 K.B. 786 CA at 795.

(v)   The distinction between acts of the claimant and acts of third parties

After para.10-061, add a new paragraph:

10-061A   In *Perry v Raleys Solicitors* [2019] UKSC 5; [2019] 2 W.L.R. 636, the claimant miner alleged that negligent advice from his solicitors had led him to settle a personal injury claim under the government scheme for general damages only, and that he had lost the opportunity of making a "services" claim under the other head of the government scheme. The services claim was dependent upon proving that the miner was unable to perform six basic domestic tasks. The trial judge rejected the miner's evidence that he had been unable to perform the six tasks. He held that the miner had not lost the opportunity of making a services claim since one could not have been honestly made. The Court of Appeal overturned this conclusion on the basis that it involved conducting a trial within a trial but the conclusion was restored by the Supreme Court. The Supreme Court endorsed the *Allied Maples* distinction that the claimant needed to prove on the balance of probabilities matters that he would have done but that he only needed to prove a loss of chance where the issue was something that would have been done by a third party (at [20]). As Lord Briggs said in delivering the decision with which the other Justices agreed, the distinction is a "sensible, fair and practicable dividing line" (at [21]). There is no impediment that this might involve a "trial within a trial" because if this issue can be tried then it should be tried. Since the trial judge concluded that the claimant could not have brought an honest claim the Supreme Court held that the trial judge was right to reject his claim.

To the end of fourth sentence, after "on third parties.", add new footnote 252a:

10-062   [252a] The proposition in this sentence endorsed by Andrew Burrows QC sitting as a High Court judge in *Palliser Ltd v Fate Ltd* [2019] EWHC 43 (QB); [2019] Lloyd's Rep. I.R. 341 at [27].

Replace para.10-064 with:

Some difficulty is encountered with the decision in *Dixon v Clement Jones Solici-* **10-064**
tors,[256] which, while looking like a run of the mill case of solicitors' negligence in
conducting litigation, yet appears to mark a departure from the application to claimants of the balance of probability rule. Mrs Dixon's action against her accountant
had been struck out for her solicitor's failure to serve a statement of claim. The accountant had negligently failed to advise her of the financial dangers of entering a
business transaction which was likely to be, and in the event proved to be, a losing
one, but the trial judge found that, on the balance of probabilities, she would have
ignored her accountant's advice and gone ahead with the transaction in any event.
This, however, did not cause her action against her solicitor to fail. The Court of
Appeal reasoned thus. While her action against her accountant would have failed
if she could not prove that, given the correct advice, she would not have gone ahead
with the transaction, it was the *chance* of whether she would have gone ahead that
was relevant in her action against the solicitor, being simply one issue within all the
other issues that had to be assessed for their prospects.[257] The trial judge had
therefore been entitled to award her damages on the basis that she had a 30 per cent
chance of succeeding against her solicitor. For the court to have decided otherwise
would have been virtually to commit it to conducting a trial within a trial which the
courts have said they do not, and must not, do.[258] Much of this reasoning can no
longer stand after the decision of the Supreme Court in *Perry v Raleys Solicitors*
[2019] UKSC 5; [2019] 2 W.L.R. 636. However, in giving the judgment of the
Supreme Court in that case, Lord Briggs pointed to a basis upon which the result
in Dixon might have been correct. Since the client had already given instructions
for the underlying claim to be brought there was "nothing which she needed to
prove that she would have done had the solicitors acted competently and served the
particulars of claim in time" (at 647 [40]). See also *Hanif v Middleweeks* [2000]
Lloyd's Rep. P.N. 920 CA and *Sharif v Garrett & Co* [2001] EWCA Civ 1269;
[2002] 1 W.L.R. 3118 which were also approved on this point in *Perry* [2019]
UKSC 5; [2019] 2 W.L.R. 636 at 646–647, [36]–[38].

[256] [2004] EWCA Civ 1005; [2005] P.N.L.R. 6 CA at 93.

[257] [2004] EWCA Civ 1005; [2005] P.N.L.R. 6 CA at [42], per Rix LJ.

[258] "It is the prospects and not the hypothetical decision in the lost trial that have to be investigated":
[2004] EWCA Civ 1005; [2005] P.N.L.R. 6 CA at 27, per Rix LJ. See too para.10-096, below.

To the start of the paragraph, add:

The correctness of His Honour Judge Hodge QC's reasoning was considered in **10-067**
Moda International Brands Ltd v Gateley LLP [2019] EWHC 1326 (QB); [2019]
P.N.L.R. 27. There, Freedman J, in a cogent judgment, after referring to parts of the
paragraphs above held that the same loss of chance approach should be taken
whether or not the third party gives evidence. He relied upon both reasons of
principle (a difference between proof by the claimant of their own likely conduct
and proof of the conduct of someone else), lack of precedent for the approach of
Judge Hodge QC, and pragmatic reasons (the artificial distinctions that could arise
concerning whether third parties are available witnesses and the different levels of
engagement by third parties): see [176].

After the paragraphs under para.10-067, add a new paragraph:

An overall summary of this entire area was made, with crystal clarity, by Andrew **10-067A**
Burrows QC sitting as a High Court judge prior to his appointment to the Supreme
Court of the United Kingdom in *Palliser Ltd v Fate Ltd* [2019] EWHC 43 (QB);

[2019] Lloyd's Rep. I.R. 341 at [27]. Summarising the principles of proof in all instances of uncertainty he said:

> "The correct picture of the law on proof in relation to damages is therefore that where the uncertainty is as to past fact, the 'all or nothing balance of probabilities' test applies. Where the uncertainty is as to the future, proportionate damages are appropriate. Where the uncertainty is as to hypothetical events, the correct test to be applied depends on the nature of the uncertainty: if it is uncertainty as to what the claimant would have done, the all or nothing balance of probabilities test applies; if it is as to what a third party would have done, damages are assessed proportionately according to the chances."

(d) Assessment of the value of the lost chance

(i) Where the chance relates to success in a damages claim

Replace para.10-101 with:

10-101   In *Charles*,[455] the taking into account of developments after the notional trial date served to increase the damages. By contrast, in *Dudarec* and again in *Whitehead* this caused the damages to be significantly smaller, if not eliminated. In a previous edition of this text the question was asked whether, if after the notional trial date for the original action a newly discovered miracle cure were to restore the claimant to his pre-accident condition or he were to meet an unexpected death, a court would be happy with the logic of awarding a whole normal lifetime of sizeable earnings and onerous medical expenses. Clearly, as *Whitehead* shows, a court would not be, and rightly so.

[455] And in the Australian and Canadian cases, and also the Scots case, cited at para.10-098, above.

Replace para.10-102 and add a new paragraph:

10-102   The difficult question is how to reconcile the competing principles that (i) damages should be assessed at the date of trial, and (ii) the absurdity in some circumstances of ignoring some events that occur after the notional trial date. In both *Dudarec* and *Whitehead* the court sought to justify its conclusion by the broad general principle that, in Harman LJ's words in *Curwen v James* [1963] 1 W.L.R. 748 CA; [1963] 2 All E.R. 619, "the court should never speculate where it knows". Yet praying in aid this principle is inappropriate in this context where the loss suffered is the quantum that would have been received on the notional settlement or trial. The issue is what was known then and not what was known when the claim against the solicitor was eventually heard. In contrast, in *Edwards v Hugh James Ford Simey (A Firm)* [2018] EWCA Civ 1299; [2018] P.N.L.R. 30 at [73] Irwin LJ (with whom Singh and Underhill LJJ agreed) held that to allow admission of subsequent evidence was exceptional, where the application of ordinary principles would not do justice between the parties. Hence, the consequences of the supervening event needed to be significant or, in the words of Underhill LJ quoting from Lord Wilberforce, an affront to common sense, or a sense of justice: [2018] EWCA Civ 1299; [2018] P.N.L.R. 30 at [78], quoting *Mulholland v Mitchell* [1971] A.C. 666 at 680. In *Edwards*, the event that was subsequent to the date of the notional trial or settlement of the solicitors' negligence in relation to claims of vibration white finger was a report by a vascular surgeon that would not have been available at a trial or settlement. The Recorder held that the report had the effect of casting such doubt upon the claims that recovery would have been less than the amount for which the claim settled, after the alleged negligence. The Court of Appeal held that the subsequent evidence did not categorically prove fraud and it was, therefore, not exceptional.

It may be that many of the exceptional cases could be rationalised on the basis **10-102A** that loss would not be assessed at the date of the notional trial or settlement where the event would have the effect that the notional trial or settlement would not have brought finality. For instance, if the event amounted to fresh evidence that would have been admissible on an appeal, or if it could amount to a ground to set aside a notional trial or settlement, then just as the trial or settlement date should not be fixed so too the date for assessment of loss should not be fixed.

(6) Where certainty as to the loss suffered is dependent on future events

After para.10-125, add a new paragraph:

The position at which we have arrived, therefore, is that although some cases **10-126** have treated the approach in *The Mihalis Angelos*, *The Golden Victory* and *Bunge SA v Nidera BV* as a general principle, not confined to anticipatory breach, other cases have effectively distinguished that trio on the basis that they concern anticipatory breach; in other cases, the usual measure of damages should not be discounted merely because the performance for which the claimant contracted might not have been provided for reasons other than the claimant's breach. The latter approach offers a principled way forward, by which damages are awarded as a measure of the value of the promised performance. Where the breach is anticipatory then the promised performance that was not provided was being ready, willing and able to perform. If that readiness, willingness or ability had been present, but the performance would not have been supplied for reasons other than breach, then the damages will be reduced or nominal. But where the breach is the failure to provide the goods or service then, in the words of Lord Reed in *Morris-Garner v One Step (Support) Ltd* [2018] UKSC 20; [2019] A.C. 649 at [35], damages are a "substitute for performance". The best illustration of this is the decision of the Court of Appeal in *Classic Maritime Inc v Limbungan Makmur Sdn Bhd* [2019] EWCA Civ 1102; [2019] 2 All E.R. (Comm) 592, a charterer was required to provide seven cargoes to the ship owner under a contract of affreightment. It provided none and was not in a position to provide any. However, the charterer relied upon a burst dam that occurred from the time that the third cargo was due. The charterer submitted that if it had been ready and willing to perform, the burst dam would have provided it with a defence under an exemptions clause so that damages should only be nominal. The trial judge, Teare J, accepted this submission. The Court of Appeal did not. It awarded almost US$20 million in damages for the five cargoes. The measure of damages was for the value of the ship owner's right to performance. As Males LJ (with whom Rose and Haddon-Cave LJJ agreed) said, the ship owner's right that was violated was its right to be provided a cargo (at [82]). As Males LJ recognised, the circumstance of anticipatory breach considered in *The Golden Victory* and *Bunge SA v Nidera BV* is different (see at [83]). In cases of anticipatory breach, the duty that the charterers breach is a duty to be ready and willing to perform. The value of that right might be negligible if performance was never going to be received for reasons other than breach.

PART 2 NON-COMPENSATORY DAMAGES

CHAPTER 13

EXEMPLARY DAMAGES

II. CASES IN WHICH EXEMPLARY DAMAGES MAY BE AWARDED

1. TYPES OF CLAIM IN WHICH EXEMPLARY DAMAGES ARE POSSIBLE

In the penultimate sentence, after "Canada v Got", remove the full stop and add:
, although the Court of Appeal in Singapore has refused to follow that approach: **13-016**
PH Hydraulics & Engineering Pte Ltd v Airtrust (Hong Kong) Ltd [2017] 2 S.L.R.
129.

After para.13-016, add a new paragraph:
Any change will need to come at the level of the Supreme Court. In *Aarons v* **13-016A**
Brocket Hall (Jersey) Ltd [2018] EWHC 222 (QB), after quoting para.13-016
above, it was rightly said by Moulder J that the mere prospect that the law might
be developed by the Supreme Court to recognise exemplary damages was not a sufficient basis to grant permission to amend so as to raise that claim (at [8]).

III. COMPUTATION OF THE EXEMPLARY AWARD

1. VARIOUS CRITERIA APPLIED BY THE COURTS

(5) The relevance of the amount awarded as compensation

After para.13-041, add a new paragraph:

13-041A   *Ramzan v Brookwide Ltd* [2010] EWHC 2453 (Ch); [2011] 2 All E.R. 38; and on appeal [2011] EWCA Civ 985; [2012] 1 All E.R. 903 CA illustrates that even a very large award of compensatory damages might not be sufficient to fulfil the purposes for which an award of exemplary damages would otherwise be awarded. In that case compensatory damages were in excess of half a million pounds yet an award of exemplary damages was made. More recently, *AXA Insurance UK Plc v Financial Claims Solutions Ltd* [2018] EWCA Civ 1330; [2019] R.T.R. 1 reaffirmed this principle in circumstances where the profit sought to be made from fraudulent insurance claims, of £85,000, would have been entirely eradicated by the award of compensation of that amount. Nevertheless, the court made an additional award of £20,000 in exemplary damages.

(6) The relevance of any criminal penalty

To the end of para.13-042, add:

13-042   And, again in *AXA Insurance UK Plc v Financial Claims Solutions Plc* [2018] EWCA Civ 1330; [2019] R.T.R. 1 at [33], the Court of Appeal held that it was not to the point that criminal proceedings had been brought against one defendant and that confiscation proceedings were pending. The assumption must have been that the confiscation proceedings would take the exemplary damages award into account in the punishment imposed.

(8) The position with multiple claimants

To the end of the paragraph, add:

13-044   In *Quinn v Ministry of Defence* [2018] NIQB 82 at [72], the criticism made in this paragraph was noted although since it was concluded (at [77]) that there was no need for deterrence the issue did not arise.

CHAPTER 14

RESTITUTIONARY DAMAGES

In the next edition the title of this chapter will be changed to

In the next edition "Negotiating Damages and User Damages".

At the beginning of the chapter, add a new part and paragraphs:

AI. THE STATE OF THE LAW AND THE NOMENCLATURE

Previous editions of this work built upon two decades of development in the area   **14-A001**
of damages which do not compensate for loss. Recent editions treated the species
of damages described as Wrotham Park damages, after the decision in *Wrotham
Park Estate Co Ltd v Parkside Homes Ltd* [1974] 1 W.L.R. 798; [1974] 2 All E.R.
321, by the name restitutionary damages. The whole of that analysis must now be
revisited in light of the decisions of the United Kingdom Supreme Court in *One Step
(Support) Ltd v Morris-Garner* [2018] UKSC 20; [2019] A.C. 649 and *Prudential
Assurance Co Ltd v Revenue and Customs Commissioners* [2018] UKSC 39; [2018]
3 W.L.R. 652.

In *Morris-Garner*, the Morris-Garners sold a business to One Step (Support) that   **14-A002**
they had previously run providing support services to vulnerable people referred by
a local council. The Morris-Garners entered a binding agreement with One Step
(Support) that for a limited period they would not engage in various forms of
competition with it. They breached that agreement in various ways. Although One

Step (Support) must have suffered some loss, the difficulty lay in proving the amount of that loss. As Lord Sumption JSC observed at [105], proof of financial loss would require it to show (i) how many customers it would have contracted with if the Morris-Garners had not breached the contract, (ii) when and for how long those contracts would have been made, (iii) the volume of business covered by those contracts, and (iv) how profitable the additional business would have been for One Step (Support).

14-A003   One Step (Support) sought damages, including in the form of "negotiating damages", being the price that a reasonable defendant would pay, and a reasonable claimant would demand, in a negotiation for release from the contractual obligations. As Lord Reed JSC (with whom Lady Hale PSC, Lord Wilson, and Lord Carnwath agreed) recognised, these damages are juridically the same as "user damages", where a defendant is required to pay a reasonable sum for the opportunity to use the benefit that the defendant obtained. Lord Reed held that damages in these cases were compensatory for One Step (Support)'s loss. He preferred to describe the damages as "negotiating damages" (at [3]). Lord Reed perceptively observed that to describe these damages as "providing compensation for loss" was to refer to loss in a sense that was not conventional (at [30]). He described the loss as the claimant's actions in "[preventing] the owner from exercising his right to obtain the economic value of the use in question" and said that the defendant should compensate the claimant because, "[p]ut shortly, he takes something for nothing, for which the owner was entitled to require payment".

14-A004   The reason why the loss of the opportunity to exercise a right to obtain the economic value of the use of an asset is unconventional is because in many of these cases, the claimant has not proved any loss in the sense of any adverse consequences actually experienced by him or her. The claimant cannot prove (i) that he or she has been financially disadvantaged, (ii) that he or she has lost any opportunity that would have been taken, or (iii) that he or she has suffered any non-financial loss of happiness, assuming that to be recoverable. The claimant, in his or her wealth and otherwise in life, might be entirely unaffected by the wrongdoing.

14-A005   Nevertheless, when the claimant has contractual or property rights, those rights can have value to both the claimant and the defendant because a demand might be made for payment in order for a release from, or licence to use, them. In the negotiating damages cases the claimant previously had an asset in the form of a valuable opportunity. Now the claimant has none. As Lord Reed observed, the loss can be said to be "the value of the right to control the use of the property as it had been wrongfully used" (at [79]). In discussing one case (*Vercoe v Rutland Fund Management Ltd* [2010] EWHC 424 (Ch); [2010] Bus. L.R. D141) Lord Reed conceptualised the loss suffered by the claimants as the loss of "a valuable opportunity to exercise their right to control the use of the information" (at [84]). Once the loss is conceptualised as a loss of an asset then it should be recovered irrespective of whether the claimant would have exercised that opportunity. In Lord Reed's words, the loss arises from the owner being prevented from "exercising his right to obtain the economic value of the use in question" (at [30]). Similarly, Lord Reed explained that the recovery of negotiating damages in *Experience Hendrix LLC v PPX Enterprises Inc* [2003] EWCA Civ 323; [2003] 1 All E.R. (Comm) 830 should be understood on the basis that the claimant was wrongfully prevented from exercising a valuable right to control the use made of PPX's copyright (at [89]) and therefore lost the asset being the valuable opportunity to require payment for a release from that control.

Recovery of negotiating damages or user damages therefore reduces to the short **14-A006** question of whether the breach of contract can be said to deprive the claimant of a valuable asset, including an opportunity, that had been created or was protected by the contractual right. A claimant's contractual right to control the use of land, intellectual property, or the confidentiality of material are all examples where the contract protects the asset which takes the form of the opportunity to control. The loss is therefore the impairment of the asset, namely the loss of the valuable opportunity to require payment for the release from the control (at [92]). In contrast, the contractual restraints in *Morris-Garner* were said to be imposed by "a commercial entity whose only interest in the defendants' performance of their obligations under the covenants was commercial" (at [98]). No separate asset of One Step (Support) had been impaired. It was entitled only to losses to be quantified based on the financial losses that it had suffered.

The difficult question for the future will be how to identify whether a claimant's **14-A007** contractual right, breached by a defendant, creates or protects a valuable asset such as an opportunity to control. A contractual right that controls the use of a tangible asset or to control confidentiality is apparently such a right. But a contractual right to restrain competition, which might be said to be a right that protects the valuable asset of goodwill, is not: see also *Keystone Healthcare Ltd v Parr* [2018] EWHC 1509 (Ch) at [225]–[227]. Perhaps the best that can be said is that a claimant will need to identify an asset over which the claimant has "exclusive dominion" (*Morris-Garner* at [110]) and goodwill is not such an asset.

The loss-based analysis of these cases is not the only way that damages of this **14-A008** nature can be conceptualised. Prior to *Morris-Garner*, one solution to the problems of calculation of loss was to recognise that, in an appropriate case, a claimant might be able to bring a claim for restitutionary damages, seeking an award of an objective measure of the gain made by the defendant rather than the loss that he or she had suffered. That objective measure is the amount that the defendant would have had to pay for the benefit in a hypothetical, reasonable negotiation. As the previous edition of this book expressed the point, the defendant had obtained a benefit by getting something for nothing. The defendant should be required to pay its reasonable value. Various cases supported this analysis. For this reason some judges insisted that these damages were awarded on restitutionary principles (see below at para.14-002).

Despite the cogency of this restitutionary damages analysis, prior to *Morris-* **14-A009** *Garner* there were cases in which some judges insisted that the negotiating damages were only compensatory for loss (see, for instance, *Jaggard v Sawyer* [1995] 1 W.L.R. 269 at 281–282 per Sir Thomas Bingham MR, with whose judgment Kennedy LJ agreed, and see paras 14-046–14-047 below). Although Lord Reed favoured an analysis of these damages as based upon loss, he did not exclude the restitutionary analysis. He said (at [79]):

"[S]ince the assessment of damages in the property cases was based on the value of the right to control the use of the property as it had been wrongfully used, there is a sense in which it can be said that the damages in those cases 'may be measured by reference to the benefit gained by the wrongdoer from the breach', provided the 'benefit' is taken to be the objective value of the wrongful use. The same can be said of the *Wrotham Park* line of cases, subject to the same proviso, and subject also to the role of equitable considerations in the making of awards under Lord Cairns' Act. The courts did not, however, adopt a benefits-based approach, but conceived of the awards as compensating for loss."

14-A010   In *Morris-Garner*, Lord Reed also spoke of the basis for these damages as a defendant taking something for nothing, reiterating similar remarks in earlier cases (including Sir Robert Megarry V-C in *Tito v Waddell (No.2)* [1977] Ch. 106 at 335 and Mance LJ in *Experience Hendrix LLC v PPX Enterprises Inc* [2003] EWCA Civ 323; [2003] 1 All E.R. (Comm) 830 at [26]). This focus upon the defendant taking something for nothing might easily have been seen as supporting the restitutionary analysis. Lord Reed's insistence at [73], correctly, that the focus is not upon the (actual) use of the benefit does not detract from this analysis because the benefit received is the valuable opportunity to take advantage of the benefit, not the actual use or manner in which the opportunity is exercised.

14-A011   In almost all cases there will be little difference between a restitutionary analysis of negotiating damages and a loss-based analysis of negotiating damages. The same emphasis on the value received by the defendant appears in intellectual property cases where the "user" principle is deployed in the calculation of damages based upon a reasonable royalty. Hence, in *Reformation Publishing Co Ltd v Cruiseco Ltd* [2018] EWHC 2761 (Ch); [2019] Bus. L.R. 78 at [51], Nugee J applied a user damages example of defendants that treated themselves as free to use certain material (*Force India Formula One Team Ltd v Aerolab SRL* [2013] EWCA Civ 780; [2013] R.P.C. 36 at [95]–[96]) to conclude that "compensation should have been assessed on the basis of the value to the defendant of the whole corpus of the information" no matter how much was actually used. Where there is a market or objective value that can be placed upon the use or the opportunity that has been wrongfully taken, then the price that a reasonable and willing buyer would pay will be the same as the price that a reasonable and willing seller would receive. As Nugee J said in *Reformation Publishing Co Ltd v Cruiseco Ltd* [2018] EWHC 2761 (Ch); [2019] Bus. L.R. 78 at [51], quoting "After all, if A wrongfully retains B's dictionary, it does not matter that he only looked up a few definitions".

14-A012   A decision given slightly before *Morris-Garner* illustrates the further difficulty that is encountered if it is concluded that an award of negotiating damages should be made. This concerns how the award should be calculated. In *National Guild of Removers & Storers Ltd v Central Moves Ltd* [2017] EWHC 3175 (IPEC) it was held by His Honour Judge Hacon that the hypothetical negotiation will not necessarily result in the price charged by a right-holder for a licence (at [47]), and in that case the hypothetical agreement was said to be that no royalty was payable (at [52]). Although there has been considerable case law concerning the different techniques for calculating the result of a hypothetical negotiation, on any view the result is not a matter of precision. The award might best be seen as one where there are a range of possible answers so that a Court of Appeal will not readily intervene. In *National Guild of Removers & Storers Ltd* at [42]–[43] it was held that this is particularly so where the decision is one of a specialist judge, such as one in the intellectual property area.

14-A013   **Remaining doubts about any restitutionary award**   Although *Morris-Garner* left some possible scope for a restitutionary damages analysis of negotiating or user damages awards, in *Prudential Assurance Co Ltd v Revenue and Customs Commissioners* [2018] UKSC 39; [2018] 3 W.L.R. 652 at [47], the Supreme Court unanimously, and baldly, stated that "user damages" awards are "designed to compensate for loss".

    The consequences of this approach will be likely to be that user damages may become far more confined than has previously been the case. An early indication of this, which arrived too late for substantial consideration in this supplement, is the decision in *Lloyd v Google LLC* [2018] EWHC 2599 (QB); [2019] 1 W.L.R. 1265, see especially [74], [76]–[81].

CHAPTER 15

DISGORGEMENT DAMAGES (ACCOUNT OF PROFITS)

TABLE OF CONTENTS

III. CIRCUMSTANCES GIVING RISE TO DISGORGEMENT DAMAGES

1. LIABILITY FOR EQUITABLE WRONGDOING

Replace para.15-008 with:

The award of disgorgement damages for equitable wrongdoing, under the label **15-008** of an account of profits, is extremely common and well-known. The account of profits "is made to provide a remedy for specific equitable wrongdoing".[22] In this edition of this work, the awards of disgorgement damages in equity will not be considered other than for breaches of fiduciary duty that arise in a contractual context. The reader is directed to the standard works on equity and trusts for a consideration of disgorgement in equity generally. It suffices to say that disgorgement of profits is available for conscious breaches of equitable duties such as breach of confidence[23] or dishonest participation in a breach of fiduciary duty.[24] This points up the current gaps in the law. It is impossible to justify the disgorgement of profits made by a dishonest assistant in a breach of fiduciary duty or a person who intentionally breaches a duty of confidence but not from a person who profits from the deceit or wilful assault of another.

[47]

²² *Glazier v Australian Men's Health (No.2)* [2001] N.S.W.S.C. 6 at [36]; see also *CMS Dolphin Ltd v Simonet* [2001] EWHC 415 (Ch); [2002] B.C.C. 600 at [97].

²³ *Attorney General v Guardian Newspapers (No.2) ("Spycatcher")* [1990] 1 A.C. 109 HL; [1988] 3 W.L.R. 776; *Keystone Healthcare Ltd v Parr* [2018] EWHC 1509 (Ch).

²⁴ *Novoship (UK) Ltd v Mikhaylyuk* [2014] EWCA Civ 908; [2015] Q.B. 499 at [71] and *Central Bank of Ecuador v Conticorp SA* [2015] UKPC 11; [2016] 1 B.C.L.C. 26 at [9]. This development was preceded in Canada and Australia by *Cook v Deeks* [1916] 1 A.C. 554 and *Warman International Ltd v Dwyer* (1995) 182 C.L.R. 544. See *Michael Wilson & Partners Ltd v Nicholls* (2011) 244 C.L.R. 427 at [106]. *Keystone Healthcare Ltd v Parr* [2018] EWHC 1509 (Ch).

2.   Liability for breach of Contract

(2)   Where there is a legitimate interest in preventing profit

*In the second paragraph of para.15-021, after "did not doubt that conclusion.",
add:*

15-021   Nor did anything said in the Supreme Court in *One Step (Support) Ltd v Morris-Garner* [2018] UKSC 20; [2018] 2 W.L.R. 1353 cast any doubt on the conclusion of the trial judge in this respect.

IV.   Measure of Profits, Causation and Remoteness of Profits

1.   Measure of Profits

Replace first paragraph with:

15-046   A preliminary question in taking an account of profits is which profits will count. Although the process of equitable accounting and how profits are determined are generally questions for accounting expertise, there are two matters of principle that should be addressed. The first is that the account of profits can include sufficiently certain anticipated profits as well as profits already made. In *Ancient Order of Foresters in Victoria Friendly Society Ltd v Lifeplan Australia Friendly Society Ltd* [2018] HCA 43; [2018] 92 A.L.J.R. 918, a majority of the High Court of Australia held that profits that can be disgorged include both profits made as well as anticipated profits to which the defendant has a right conditional upon performance.

> "To confine the account in this way would sever the process of accounting for, and disgorgement of, profit from its rationale in the principle of ensuring that the wrongdoer should not be permitted to gain from the wrongdoing" *Ancient Order of Foresters in Victoria Friendly Society Ltd v Lifeplan Australia Friendly Society Ltd* [2018] HCA 43; [2018] 92 A.L.J.R. 918 at [24]; see also *Potton Ltd v Yorkclose Ltd* [1990] F.S.R. 11 at 15.

One further matter of principle is that the profit with which disgorgement awards are concerned is the net profit actually made and not the expense which is saved by choosing a wrongful, not a proper, action. As a matter of principle it might be thought difficult to separate the two since an expense saved *is* profit made or loss reduced by acting in the wrongful manner rather than acting properly. But courts have refused, on pragmatic grounds, to make an award on the basis of an expense saved.[150] The best attempt to provide a reason for this was given by the Australian judge, McHugh J in *Dart Industries Inc v Decor Corp Pty Ltd*[151]:

> "In a litigious world of unlimited time and resources, the best approach for determining the profit derived from the infringement might be to estimate the profit of the product after allowing a proportion of the overheads and then deduct the opportunity cost of produc-

ing the infringing product. This would show the true gain of the infringer from producing or distributing the infringing product instead of the next best alternative. Another but
less exact method of determining the profit and preventing the unjust enrichment of the
infringer might be to determine what was the best alternative open to the infringer,
determine what gross revenue would have been obtained from that alternative, and deduct
that sum from the gross revenue obtained from the infringing product. Another suggested method is that there should be a deduction for that part of the overhead which
would have been absorbed in producing or selling the alternative to the extent that it was
used in producing or selling the infringing product. But to adopt any of these methods
would make an often complex subject more complex than it already is. Very likely, it
would increase the prospect of contested litigation over the taking of the account and the
cost and length of the hearing while the parties and their witnesses investigated and
debated the hypothetical ... Lindley LJ, who knew more about accounts of profits than
most lawyers, once said ... that he did 'not know any form of account which (was) more
difficult to work out, or may be more difficult to work out than an account of profits'. The
Court should be slow to adopt a rule which might increase that difficulty."

[150] See *Potton Ltd v Yorkclose Ltd* [1990] F.S.R. 11; *Peter Pan Manufacturing Corp v Corsets Silhouette
Ltd* [1964] 1 W.L.R. 96; [1963] 3 All E.R. 402; *Siddell v Vickers* (1888) 16 R.P.C. 416; *Celanese
International Corp v BP Chemicals Ltd* [1999] R.P.C. 203; *Cala Homes Ltd v Alfred McAlpine Ltd*
[1996] F.S.R. 36 at 44.

[151] (1993) 179 C.L.R. 101 at 125.

2. Scope of duty, causation and remoteness

To the end of the paragraph, add:

In *Ancient Order of Foresters in Victoria Friendly Society Ltd v Lifeplan* **15-049**
Australia Friendly Society Ltd [2018] HCA 43; [2018] 92 A.L.J.R. 918, a majority
of the High Court of Australia rejected a submission that knowing participants in
a breach of fiduciary duty did not have to disgorge profits because the profits were
said to have arisen indirectly and thus not to have been caused by the breach. It was
sufficient to say that the profit would not have been made but for the dishonest
wrongdoing, although as with cases of causation in relation to compensation in the
law of torts, where the profits are made dishonestly a defendant cannot avoid liability to disgorge profits dishonestly made by showing that those profits might have
been made honestly (at [9]). English courts have gone further when considering the
disgorgement of profits for breach of fiduciary duty. In *Parr v Keystone Healthcare*
[2019] EWCA Civ 1246; [2019] 4 W.L.R. 99 at [18], Lewison LJ, with whom Mc-
Combe and Bean LJJ agreed, held that causation was not required for any case of
breach of fiduciary duty. The requirement is only for the requirements of scope of
duty, considered below, of "some reasonable connection" or a "reasonable relationship" between the breach of duty and the profit: see *Murad v Al-Saraj* [2005]
EWCA Civ 959; [2005] W.T.L.R. 1573 at [112]; *CMS Dolphin Ltd v Simonet* [2001]
EWHC 415 (Ch); [2002] B.C.C. 600 at [97]; *Ultraframe (UK) Ltd v Fielding* [2005]
EWHC 1638 (Ch); [2007] W.T.L.R. 835 at [1588]. In other words, courts will never
refuse an order for disgorgement of profits for breach of fiduciary duty if those
profits would have been made without the breach of fiduciary duty: see *Gwembe
Valley Development Co Ltd v Koshy* [2003] EWCA Civ 1048; [2004] B.C.L.C. 131;
Murad v Al-Saraj [2005] EWCA Civ 959; [2005] W.T.L.R. 1573 at [76].

To the end of the paragraph, add:

This decision was cited with approval by the High Court of Australia in *Ancient* **15-053**
*Order of Foresters in Victoria Friendly Society Ltd v Lifeplan Australia Friendly
Society Ltd* [2018] HCA 43; [2018] 92 A.L.J.R. 918; 360 A.L.R. 1 at [15], where

it was also held that the onus is upon the party that is liable to account for profits to establish that they are too remote. In that case, the appellant company was a knowing participant in a breach of fiduciary duty by former employees of the respondent company who joined the appellant company and enticed employees of their old employer to it by means that included breaches of fiduciary duties. The new company was required to account for all of the profits made.

CHAPTER 16

LIQUIDATED DAMAGES

After para.16-002, add a new paragraph:

There is, however, always an anterior question to ask before considering whether **16-002A** a clause is for liquidated damages or for a penalty. The question is whether the clause applies to the circumstances. This is particularly important where the breach of contract consists of a failure to complete, but the clause is concerned with liquidated damages for delay. An example is the decision in *Triple Point Technology Inc v PTT Public Co Ltd* [2019] EWCA Civ 230; [2019] 1 W.L.R. 3549. Triple Point was a service provider which failed to perform any milestones for payment other than the first two. This led to termination of the contract. It failed in its claim to recover payment for the subsequent milestones that it did not complete. A counterclaim was brought by PTT for damages for breach of contract and "delay".

PTT recovered for delay in relation to the first two milestones. But a major issue was whether the clause applied to failures to complete the later milestones. The liquidated damages clause for delay provided for damages calculated at a rate per day from the due date until the date that the work was "accepted" (which must have meant "accepted from Triple Point"). The Court of Appeal, Sir Rupert Jackson (Floyd and Lewison LJJ agreeing), relied upon a decision of the House of Lords, from Scotland, which held that a similar provision did not entitle a contractor to liquidated damages for delay where the contractor never completed the work (*British Glanzstoff Manufacturing Co Ltd v General Accident, Fire and Life Assurance Co. Ltd* 1912 S.C. 591; 1912 1 S.L.T. 282 (Court of Session) and [1913] A.C. 143; 1913 S.C. (HL) 1). As Sir Rupert Jackson observed, it can be

"artificial and inconsistent with the parties' agreement to categorise the employer's losses as £x per week up to a specified date and then general damages thereafter".

Perhaps more fundamentally, the premise of the clause was that the work by Triple Point would ultimately be accepted by PTT. The whole purpose of the clause was to liquidate damages for delay in completion. It was not to liquidate damages for failure to complete. Although, as Sir Rupert Jackson rightly said, every contractual term must be interpreted in its own context (at [110]), the decision of the Court of Appeal must cast serious doubt upon earlier authorities that had allowed liquidated damages clauses to operate for delays until the point of termination (*Greenore Port Ltd v Technical & General Guarantee Co Ltd* [2006] EWHC 3119 (TCC); *Shaw v MFP Foundations and Pilings Ltd* [2010] EWHC 1839 (TCC); *Hall v Van Der Heiden (No.2)* [2010] EWHC 586 (TCC); *Bluewater Energy Services BV v Mercon Steel Structures BV* [2014] EWHC 2132 (TCC); 155 Con. L.R. 85; *GPP Big Field LLP v Solar EPC Solutions SL* [2018] EWHC 2866 (Comm).

1.   HISTORICAL DEVELOPMENT OF LIQUIDATED DAMAGES AND PENALTIES

(3)   The criterion of the intention of the parties

Replace para.16-007 with:

16-007   For a time the courts attempted to justify their interference in these contracts by stating that they were implementing the intention of the parties. Such a claim required them to look to the terminology used in the contract. The contract in *Astley v Weldon*,[22] itself had used neither the term "liquidated damages" nor the term "penalty" but soon after in *Smith v Dickenson*,[23] a clause was held to be a penalty because, it was said, the use of that term clearly prevented the court from holding that the provision was for liquidated damages, while conversely, in *Reilly v Jones*,[24] it was said that no case had been adduced in which a clause had been held to be a penalty where the parties had used the terminology of liquidated damages. However, when in 1829 in *Kemble v Farren*,[25] another milestone case, an amount expressed to be liquidated damages by the parties was held to be a penalty by the court, the bankruptcy of such an interpretation was clear. This, however, was only slowly realised,[26] and, furthermore, there was as yet no clearly developed test to take the place of the test of the parties' intention. As Rigby LJ said at the end of the 19th century in *Willson v Love*[27]:

"The history of the decisions appears to me to lead to the conclusion that the courts made a mistake when they departed in regard to these cases from the general rule that effect ought to be given to the terms of the agreement entered into by the parties, and that, when once the rule was departed from, it became extremely difficult to arrive at any clear rule on the subject."

And, indeed, the numerous 19th century cases show some confusion and not infrequent difficulty in reconciling,[28] a factor which must be recognised when relying on them as precedents. Perhaps today they are of real value only as illustrations of type-situations.[29] It is well-established today that the description in the contract of a sum due is relevant but not conclusive: *Cavendish Square Holdings BV v Makdessi* [2015] UKSC 67; [2016] A.C. 1172 at [15] and see below at para.16-019.

[22] 126 E.R. 1318; (1801) 2 Bos. & P. 346.

[23] 127 E.R. 339; (1804) 3 Bos. & P. 630.

[24] 130 E.R. 122; (1823) 1 Bing. 302.

[25] 130 E.R. 1234; (1829) 6 Bing. 141.

[26] Thus a decade later the court in *Boys v Ancell* 132 E.R. 1149; (1839) 5 Bing. N.C. 390 was still paying close attention to the terminology.

[27] [1896] 1 Q.B. 626 CA at 633.

[28] This confusion is epitomised by the different approach taken by the members of the Court of Appeal, particularly James LJ, in *Re Newman* (1876) L.R. 4 Ch. D. 724 CA and, soon after, by the members of the Court of Appeal, particularly Sir George Jessel MR, in *Wallis v Smith* (1882) L.R. 21 Ch. D. 243 CA.

[29] See paras 16-061 to 16-098, below.

2. NATURE AND EFFECT OF LIQUIDATED DAMAGES AND PENALTIES

(1) Nature of liquidated damages and penalties

(a) A summary of the test for a penalty

Replace list with:

(1) A clause can only be a penalty if it operates conditionally upon breach of **16-014** contract, in other words if it is a secondary obligation arising upon breach.

(2) Whether a clause operates conditionally upon a breach of contract is a question of substance, not form, and drafting techniques by the parties may not be effective if the true construction of a clause is that it is conditional upon breach.

(3) A penalty is not confined to the payment of money; it can include the transfer of property but it will not include cases where a proprietary or possessory right is transferred but is defeasible upon breach. The only action available in those cases is for relief against forfeiture.

(4) The question whether a clause is a penalty should be asked before asking whether relief against forfeiture should be granted. This is because the penalties doctrine operates at the time the clause comes into operation, not at the time of breach. However, it would be foolish not to plead these doctrines as defences in the alternative to a claim for forfeiture.

(5) The test for whether a clause, conditional on breach, is a penalty is whether it imposes a detriment on the contract-breaker out of all proportion to any legitimate interest of the innocent party in the enforcement of the primary obligation.

(6) In applying this test, courts should first identify the legitimate interest of the

innocent party that is being protected by the clause: *Vivienne Westwood v Conduit Street* [2017] EWHC 350 (Ch); [2017] L. & T.R. 23 at [41]; *Cargill International Trading Pte Ltd v Uttam Galva Steels Ltd* [2019] EWHC 476 (Comm) at [48]. Then, in assessing whether the provision is out of all proportion to that legitimate interest, courts should consider the circumstances in which the contract was made. A negotiated contract between properly advised parties of comparable bargaining power involves a strong initial presumption that the parties are the best judges of what is legitimate in a provision dealing with the consequences of breach.

(7) Once a clause is recognised as a penalty then the consequences are that it is void. There is no power for the court partially to enforce the clause to the extent that it might not have been penal, or to enforce it only on terms. To do so would be to rewrite the contract.

(b) The requirement of a breach of contract

To the start of the paragraph, add:

16-017 The requirement of a breach of contract has been described as a "threshold issue": *Vivienne Westwood v Conduit Street* [2017] EWHC 350 (Ch); [2017] L. & T.R. 23 at [41]; *Cargill International Trading Pte Ltd v Uttam Galva Steels Ltd* [2019] EWHC 476 (Comm) at [48].

3. RULES FOR DISTINGUISHING LIQUIDATED DAMAGES FROM PENALTIES

(1) The wording used by the parties is of marginal importance

Replace footnote 113 with:

16-029 [113] Of course, before *Kemble v Farren* 130 E.R. 1234; (1829) 6 Bing. 141 there had been decisions where the terminology was controlling, e.g. *Smith v Dickenson* 127 E.R. 339; (1804) 3 Bos. & P. 630, at para.16-007, above. See *Triple Point Technology Inc v PTT Public Co Ltd* [2019] EWCA Civ 230; [2019] 1 W.L.R. 3549 at [71].

4. APPLICATION OF THE "LEGITIMATE INTEREST" TEST

(a) Where there is only a single obligation upon the breach of which the sum becomes payable or the property transferrable

(i) Where the loss is reasonably calculable at the time of contracting

After para.16.043, add a new paragraph:

16-043A A good example, after *Makdessi*, of a valid clause that provided for payment of a larger sum upon default in the payment of a smaller sum is *Holyoake v Candy* [2017] EWHC 3397 (Ch). In that case, the contract provided for the repayment of the whole of the interest that would have been due after two years if the loan was redeemed early. The early redemption was not a breach. However, if the borrower breached the contract and defaulted then the whole of the interest would also fall due. The lender had a legitimate interest in imposing this consequence. As Nugee J said (at [471])

> "it would be surprising if by defaulting on his obligations, he could be liable for a lesser sum than if he simply wished to repay early."

(ii)   Where the loss is not reasonably calculable at the time of contracting

After para.16-046, add a new paragraph:

Another common circumstance is where, as in cases like *Lordsvale Finance Plc*   **16-046A**
v Bank of Zambia [1996] Q.B. 752; [1996] 3 W.L.R. 688, the "loss" is the greater
credit risk that a borrower has become after default, reflecting the lower value of
the creditor's loan. In *Lordsvale*, the creditor had a legitimate interest in reflecting
that consequence with an increased interest rate. In *ZCCM Investments Holdings
Plc v Konkola Copper Mines Plc* [2017] EWHC 3288 (Comm), the creditor
reflected that consequence with both interest payable at LIBOR plus 10% as well
as an acceleration of all future payments to be immediately payable. This
consequence, probably very close to the borderline, was held, by Lionel Persey QC,
sitting as a judge of the High Court, to be legitimate in circumstances in which rates
of up to 14% were paid in relation to related loans, and acceleration clauses have
long been treated as legitimate: *The Angelic Star* [1988] 1 Lloyd's Rep. 122 CA at
126. And in *Cargill International Trading Pte Ltd v Uttam Galva Steels Ltd* [2019]
EWHC 476 (Comm), Bryan J upheld as liquidated damages a clause providing for
12% interest above LIBOR in circumstances where the relevant market was in
India, the party alleging that the clause was a penalty had borrowings from 7%
above LIBOR, and there was evidence of even higher market rates.

CHAPTER 17

VINDICATORY DAMAGES

TABLE OF CONTENTS

2.   VINDICATORY DAMAGES FOR INFRINGEMENT OF A RIGHT GENERALLY

After para.17-016, add a new paragraph:

Whether nominal, or not, damages are awarded under the *Lumba* principle will **17-016A**
depend upon the counterfactual to be applied. It must be shown that the claimant
would have, not could have, been lawfully imprisoned in any event: *Parker v Chief
Constable of Essex Police* [2018] EWCA Civ 2788; [2019] 1 W.L.R. 2238 and see
R. (Kambadzi) v Secretary of State for the Home Department [2011] UKSC 23;
[2011] 1 W.L.R. 1299 at [89] (Lord Kerr). See also at [60] (Lord Hope), [77]
(Baroness Hale); *Bostridge v Oxleas NHS Foundation Trust* [2015] EWCA Civ 79;
(2015) 18 C.C.L. Rep. 144 at [23], [32], [33]. It is not even enough that one cause
of the imprisonment was the decision of the claimant, provided that it was reasonable, not to seek release on unconditional bail: *R. (Belfken) v Secretary of State for
the Home Department* [2017] EWHC 1834 (Admin) at [68]–[74]. But if the
imprisonment of the claimant would have occurred lawfully, but that the imprisonment would only have been lawful at a later time, and hence for a shorter dura-
tion, then substantial damages might be payable for the intermediate period. The
importance of focusing upon when lawful conduct would have led to imprisonment is illustrated by *Parker v Chief Constable of Essex Police* [2018] EWCA Civ
2788; [2019] 1 W.L.R. 2238. In that case, the question was whether substantial damages were payable to the claimant, better known by his stage name as Michael Bar-
rymore, when he was arrested contrary to the requirements of PACE (Police and
Criminal Evidence Act 1984). At first instance, Stuart-Smith J held that the possible counterfactuals included that (i) he would not have been arrested; (ii) he would
have been arrested but by another officer who also contravened PACE; or (iii) that
he would have been arrested lawfully (see [2017] EWHC 2140 (QB) at [52]). The
Court of Appeal rejected the second counter-factual applied by Stuart-Smith J. The
counter-factual enquiry should always concern what would have happened if the
defendant had acted lawfully ([2018] EWCA Civ 2788; [2019] 1 W.L.R. 2238 at
[104]). It is not concerned with the range of other unlawful things that a defendant
might have done. Since Mr Parker would still have been lawfully arrested, only
nominal damages were payable.

PART 3 VARIOUS GENERAL FACTORS IN THE ASSESSMENT OF DAMAGES

CHAPTER 19

THE AWARDING OF INTEREST

III.   THE POSITION AFTER SEMPRA METALS

1.   THE DECISION

Replace para.19-061 and then add a new paragraph:

19-061   Before their Lordships there was not only a claim to recover compound interest as damages but also a claim to recover compound interest as restitution for unjust enrichment. The restitutionary cause of action was in the vanguard since the claimant Sempra was said to prefer it[213] because it presented fewer limitation problems.[214] A majority of the Supreme Court allowed the restitutionary award of compound interest. The consequences of this decision turned out to be very significant. The impact of only one subsequent test case was estimated to be around £17 billion: *Prudential Assurance Co Ltd v Revenue and Customs Commissioners* [2018] UKSC 39; [2018] 3 W.L.R. 652 at [66], referring to *Littlewoods Ltd v Revenue and Customs Commissioners* [2017] UKSC 70; [2018] A.C. 869. The decision in *Sempra Metals* on the restitutionary award of compound interest was overruled in *Prudential Assurance Co Ltd v Revenue and Customs Commissioners* [2018] UKSC 39; [2018] 3 W.L.R. 652 where a unanimous Supreme Court held that a defendant was not unjustly enriched "at the expense of" the claimant merely by having the opportunity to use a capital sum. The enrichment that was "transferred from" or "at the expense of" the claimant was the capital sum only. There was no subsequent transfer of the use of that capital sum: at [71]; see also *Investment Trust Companies v Revenue and Customs Commissioners* [2017] UKSC 29; [2018] A.C. 275 at [42].

[213]   [2007] UKHL 34; [2008] 1 A.C. 561 at [18], per Lord Hope.

[214]   See [2007] UKHL 34; [2008] 1 A.C. 561 per Lord Hope at [16] and [21], and per Lord Mance at [192] and [229].

19-061A   We are not concerned with the unjust enrichment claim but with the damages claim upon which there was unanimity in *Sempra*, and which the Supreme Court declined to consider, because it was not in issue, in *Prudential Assurance Co Ltd v Revenue and Customs Commissioners* [2018] UKSC 39; [2018] 3 W.L.R. 652 at [44]. In *Sempra*, Lord Nicholls concluded his detailed examination of the law on the damages aspect of the case with:

> "I consider the court has a common law jurisdiction to award interest, simple and compound, as damages on claims for non-payment of debts as well as on other claims for breach of contract and in tort"[215]

while Lord Scott expressed his concurrence with the conclusion, which appeared to him to have been unanimously accepted, that

> "interest losses caused by a breach of contract or by a tortious wrong should be held to be in principle recoverable, but subject to proof of loss, remoteness of damage rules, obligations to mitigate damage and any other relevant rules relating to the recovery of alleged losses."[216]

[215]   [2007] UKHL 34; [2008] 1 A.C. 561 at [100].

[216]   [2007] UKHL 34; [2008] 1 A.C. 561 at [132].

3. THE RESULTS

(a) Cases where compound interest is sought

Replace para.19-068 with:

A further word should be said here about compound interest in equity today. **19-068**
Equity has shown itself prepared to award compound interest in order to ensure that
a person does not make a profit from his own wrongdoing if that person is in a
fiduciary position.[238] Such a recovery of interest constitutes an accounting or is by
way of disgorgement and is considered in Chapter 15. More uncertain is whether
there is jurisdiction in equity to award compound interest against those obtaining
money or other benefit through fraud. In Australia, the availability of disgorgement of compound interest for deceit or fraud, whether at common law or in equity,
has been accepted: *Northern Territory v Mr A Griffiths (deceased) and Lorraine
Jones on behalf of the Ngaliwurru and Nungali Peoples* [2019] HCA 7; [2019] 93
A.L.J.R. 327 at [131], [340]. In England, it has also been accepted recently that
disgorgement of profits made as compound interest is possible in relation to
compound interest made by a dishonest recipient in breach of fiduciary duty: *FM
Capital Partners Ltd v Marino* [2019] EWHC 725 (Comm) at [33]. See also *Central
Bank of Ecuador v Conticorp SA* [2015] UKPC 11; [2016] 1 B.C.L.C. 26 at [185]
referring to *Novoship v Nikitin* [2014] EWCA Civ 908; [2015] Q.B. 499. It is hard
to see why it should be available in such circumstances but not in relation to actual
fraud either at common law or in equity. The question was raised but left undecided
by the Court of Appeal in *Clef Aquitaine SARL v Laporte Materials (Barrow) Ltd*,[239]
though it was accepted that the matter will need decision one day.[240] A decision in
favour would in effect be allowing compound interest upon compensation rather
than as disgorgement, being similar to compensation for fraudulent misrepresenta-
tion, but historically speaking the award would need to be classified as one not for
damages but for equitable compensation so as to attract the equitable jurisdiction.
Since *Clef Aquitaine* the question has reappeared more than once but with no very
clear answer. In *Black v Davies*,[241] which was an action in deceit, McCombe J would
have been prepared to award compound interest but for his belief that the equitable
remedy of compound interest should be ancillary to an equitable cause of action.
Instead, the Court of Appeal, while not sharing this belief, refused compound interest because the defendant's fraudulent representation had not caused him to obtain
and retain money belonging to the claimants but had simply caused them to lose
money.[242] Subsequently, an award of compound interest was made in the
complicated fraud case of *Man Nutzfahrzeuge AG v Freightliner Ltd*,[243] but it is not
entirely clear whether this was based on the benefit obtained by the fraudulent
defendant or on the loss to the claimant.[244] Or, now, to the date of payment if before
judgment: see para.19-040, above. Again, in *Glenn v Watson* [2018] EWHC 2483
(Ch), Nugee J awarded compound interest upon a claim based upon deceit but the
claim, which was expressed as one for "equitable compensation" consequent upon
a constructive trust of the money paid by deceit, bore a close resemblance to
restitution. These difficulties of where exactly equity lies in this area of damages
can now be by-passed, it is suggested, by applying *Sempra Metals* so as to allow,
where appropriate, compound interest at common law in deceit actions.

[238] See especially the treatment of the interest issue by Buckley LJ in *Wallersteiner v Moir (No.2)* [1975]
Q.B. 373 CA at 397 to 399, and by Hobhouse J and Lord Browne-Wilkinson in *Westdeutschebank
Landesbank Girozentrale v Islington Borough Council* at, respectively, [1994] 4 All E.R. 972, 990 to
995 and [1996] A.C. 669, 701D. See too *O'Sullivan v Management Agency and Music* [1985] Q.B. 428;

[1984] 3 W.L.R. 448 and see *Miliangos v George Frank (Textiles) (No.2)* [1977] Q.B. 489 at 495A to D, per Bristow J.

239 [2001] Q.B. 488; [2000] 3 W.L.R. 1760.

240 [2001] Q.B. 448 at 503H to 506B.

241 [2004] EWHC 1464 (QB).

242 See [2005] EWCA Civ 531, especially at [87]–[89].

243 [2005] EWHC 2347 (Comm).

244 See [2005] EWHC 2347 (Comm) at [318]–[321]. The claim in deceit, and therefore the issue of interest, does not appear in the appeal at [2008] P.N.L.R. 6 at 117.

IV. CALCULATION OF THE AMOUNT OF INTEREST

2. RATE OF INTEREST AWARDED

(2)   Cases in the Commercial Court and analogous cases

(d)   Deviations from the commercial rate

(ii)   Special investment account rate

Replace footnote 541 with:

19-119   541 Interest is dealt with at [2000] Lloyd's Rep. P.N. 404 at 408–410. But without reasons he reverted to judgment debt rate in *Hamilton-Jones v David & Snape* [2003] EWHC 3147 (Ch); [2004] 1 W.L.R. 924. Not doubted on this point on appeal in *Perry v Raleys Solicitors* [2019] UKSC 5; [2019] 2 W.L.R. 636.

CHAPTER 21

COSTS, DAMAGES AND FINES IN PREVIOUS PROCEEDINGS

TABLE OF CONTENTS

II.   Costs in Previous Proceedings between the Same Parties

2.   Further Proceedings where a Separate Independent Cause of Action is
Available

(1)   Tort

After para.21-023, add a new paragraph:

Deceit   In *Playboy Club London Ltd v Banca Nazionale Del Lavora Spa* [2019]   **21-023A**
EWHC 303 (Comm); [2019] L.L.R. 538 the question arose in the context of an application for permission to amend particulars of claim in an action based on deceit.
The Club had failed in an action for negligence against the bank, with costs against
the Club, because the bank had only assumed responsibility to the agent that the
Club used for the confidential reference without disclosing the Club's identity as
principal (*Banca Nazionale del Lavoro SPA v Playboy Club London Ltd* [2018]

UKSC 43; [2018] 1 W.L.R. 4041). The Club then commenced an action for deceit which the Court of Appeal, reversing the trial judge, held not to be an abuse of process. A preliminary issue was whether on the claim for deceit the Club could recover, as its loss, the legal costs that it had been ordered to pay to the bank. The bank submitted that no court had ever made an award of costs as part of an award of damages which effectively reversed a previous costs award by allowing the costs (a) of a previous legal action (b) between the same parties (c) in which the claiming party was unsuccessful and had costs awarded against it. It is true that in *Dadourian Group International v Simms* [2009] EWCA Civ 169; [2009] 1 Lloyd's Rep. 601, the award of costs as damages was made where the parties were not the same as those in the previous proceedings and *Berry v British Transport Commission* [1962] 1 Q.B. 306; [1961] 3 W.L.R. 450 involved an original case which was criminal. But the principle should be the same, as senior counsel for the Playboy Club explained, in reliance upon the discussion in this chapter of the 20th edition of this work (see at [40]).

The Deputy High Court judge rightly concluded that this was a matter that ought to be decided in light of all the findings at trial. As a matter of principle, the only obstacle should be whether the legal system would stultify itself if it were to order one party to pay costs only later to allow that party to recover those costs as part of its loss. The answer to that question is resolved by the determination that the second action is not an abuse of process. If it is legitimate for fresh litigation to agitate a new claim even though the new claim might have led to a different overall result in the earlier proceedings, then there is no more a contradiction with the earlier proceedings by allowing a recovery of costs paid than it is to make orders that differ from those that were made in the original proceedings.

BREACH OF UNDERTAKINGS AS TO DAMAGES

Replace paras 22-004–22-006, and then add new paragraphs:

3.   THE ASSESSMENT OF DAMAGES UPON AN ENFORCED UNDERTAKING

22-004 The most comprehensive consideration of this issue came in the decision in *Fiona Trust & Holding Corp v Privalov (No.2)* [2016] EWHC 2163 (Comm); [2017] 2 All E.R. 570, as it was named at first instance. That decision has now been appealed, and is now named *SCF Tankers Ltd v Privalov* [2017] EWCA Civ 1877; [2018] 1 W.L.R. 5623, after Fiona Trust changed its name. Although the decision below was approved, the Court of Appeal added a number of helpful remarks which prompt some substantial additions and revisions as follows to the text of this chapter. The Fiona Trust parties were 76 related company claimants who brought claims against Mr Nikitin and his companies for an amount in excess of US $577 million. At the outset of the litigation, the Fiona Trust parties obtained a worldwide freezing order in respect of assets up to the value of $225 million. The freezing order was discharged shortly afterwards when the Nikitin parties gave security undertakings in order to obtain the discharge. The Fiona Trust parties gave the usual undertakings as to damages in order to obtain the freezing order and the consequential security undertakings. However, the usual terms of the undertaking, which permit transactions in the ordinary course of business, was qualified to provide that the sale and purchase of vessels and other specified matters was not in the ordinary course of business. The outcome of the trial was that most of the claims were dismissed. The primary judge, Andrew Smith J, ordered an inquiry as to the damages suffered by the defendants as a result of the freezing orders and security undertakings. He concluded that the findings about Mr Nikitin's dishonesty and misconduct did not preclude the Nikitin parties from recovering damages on the breach of the undertaking. In other words, his discretion was exercised to order an inquiry as to damages. Although there is a discretion to order the inquiry, the calculation of, and rules concerning, damages are not discretionary.

22-005 The inquiry as to damages was undertaken by Males J. The ultimate result of the inquiry was an award of $59.8 million in damages, based on the undertaking as to damages. The appeal from that decision was dismissed. Males J concluded, in findings not disturbed on the appeal, that: (i) the Nikitin parties were prohibited by terms of the undertakings from concluding "newbuilding" contracts that they would otherwise have undertaken with Korean shipbuilding yards; (ii) this caused the Nikitin parties a loss that was not too remote; and (iii) there was neither a "break in the causal chain" nor a failure to mitigate by the failure of the Nikitin parties to make a "far from straightforward" application for the release of the secured funds to make a purchase, which application would have been vigorously resisted and which faced forensic obstacles from a reasonable assessment of the approach of Judge Mackie QC at prior security hearings.

22-006   Males J held, and there was rightly no dispute on appeal, that the damages on the undertaking for the losses from the freezing orders must be assessed by reference to ordinary contractual principles, including principles of causation, mitigation and remoteness. However, as Males J recognised, although the same principles will generally apply, the analogy with breach of contract is not exact. The undertaking is given to the Court although it remains a promise for the benefit of the other party. Males J also held that since the assessment of damages suffered as a result of a freezing order is often "inherently imprecise", a "liberal assessment" of the defendants' damages should be adopted (at [51]). The expression "liberal assessment" is probably best avoided because it carries the false implication that the imprecision of facts permits the application of principles which are more generous than they would be in relation to any other enforced promise.

22-006A   **Loss of a chance**   The difficulty in calculation in *Fiona Trust* was that it was not certain that the Nikitin parties would have realised a profit by investing the assets that were the subject of the freezing order: there was a boom in the shipping market from 2005 to mid-2008, followed by a crash of unprecedented severity. This is not a difficulty unique to cases involving calculation of damages which flow from an undertaking. The same issue often arises in loss of chance cases. As Males J recognised at first instance, referring to the recovery in some cases of profits quantified on the basis of a lost chance:

> "The true position is that in principle damages can be awarded for loss of profits even if a claimant might have made a loss. The approach which the court will adopt is to ask whether the claimant has proved to a sufficient standard (which may be the balance of probabilities, or sometimes merely that there was a real and substantial chance as in loss of a chance cases) that its trading would have been profitable. If so, the court will make the best assessment of the damages that it can, applying if necessary a discount to reflect whatever uncertainty exists, while recognising that a party seeking to show what might have happened is not required to perform an impossible task with unrealistic precision." (at [55].)

Of course, Males J could not have meant to suggest that there are competing standards of balance of probabilities and real and substantial chance. More accurately, there is a single standard of balance of probabilities but a claimant is entitled to a quantified loss of chance by proving, to that standard, that there was a real and substantial chance which was lost.

22-006B   **Causation and remoteness**   As to these issues, the same principles apply as for a breach of contract. The Court of Appeal in *SCF Tankers Ltd v Privalov* held that a claim for damages for breach of the undertaking requires proof that the damage would not have occurred but for the injunction: [2017] EWCA Civ 1877; [2018] 1 W.L.R. 5623 at [41]. As to how "but for" causation should be proved, the Court of Appeal adopted an earlier approach of Saville J, which was itself approved on appeal (see *Financiera Avenida v Shiblaq*, transcript 7 November 1990, cited at [2017] EWCA Civ 1877; [2018] 1 W.L.R. 5623 at [43]), that causation can be proved by establishing "a prima facie case that the damage was exclusively caused by the relevant order". The adoption of this approach should not be taken to be a suggestion that but for causation can only be proved by establishing a prima facie case that the damage was an exclusive cause. The requirement of but for causation can be established by any forensic technique inviting that inference. Further, the Court of Appeal could not have intended that "exclusive cause" be treated literally because in life everything is the result of multiple causes. Rather, the Court of Appeal must have been suggesting that the order was so significant to the damage that it could be practically treated as being to the exclusion of other contributing reasons.

As with the usual approach to mitigation, the onus is upon the party who obtained the freezing order to demonstrate a failure to mitigate. In *SCF Tankers Ltd v Privalov*, Males J and the Court of Appeal (Beatson LJ; Lewison and Kitchin LJJ agreeing) both rejected the submission that the Nikitin parties had failed to mitigate because they did not apply to the court for the release of funds from the security undertaking in order to make a purchase. As Males J explained at [48], the potentially catastrophic effect of the "nuclear weapon" of a freezing order requires courts to take a realistic approach to a submission that a defendant should have made an application to the court for a variation of the freezing order. This nuclear weapon having been deployed by the court upon the defendant's initiative (rather than, for instance, an order merely requiring notification to the claimant in advance of expenditure), it might be reasonable for a claimant not even to attempt an application for variation which is often "far from straightforward": [2016] EWHC 2163 (Comm); [2017] 2 All E.R. 570 at [48], quoting *Abbey Forwarding Ltd (In Liquidation) v Hone (No.3)* [2014] EWCA Civ 711; [2015] Ch. 309 at [65]. **22-006C**

As for remoteness of damage, again consistently with the usual approach, the party seeking damages must establish that they are not too remote. This is generally done, again consistently with the cases on remoteness of damage, by showing that the type of loss is known or within the reasonable contemplation of the parties. Again, consistently with the usual remoteness principle that it is not necessary to contemplate the particular extent of loss provided that the loss is usual or reasonably contemplated, the decision in *SCF Tankers Ltd v Privalov* demonstrates also that there is a basic difference between, on the one hand, losses that are uncertain but usual and, on the other hand, losses that are unusual (at [57]). **22-006D**

PART 4 PARTICULAR CONTRACTS AND TORTS

CHAPTER 24

THE MEASURE OF DAMAGES IN CONTRACT AND TORT COMPARED

After para.24-013, add a new paragraph:

Another example of a concurrent liability in contract and tort based upon the **24-013A** same assumption of responsibility can be seen in *ARB v IVF Hammersmith Ltd* [2017] EWHC 2438 (QB); [2018] 2 W.L.R. 1223, where a claim for damages against a fertility clinic was unsuccessful. The claim was brought for breach of an implied contractual duty to take care but it could equally have been brought in tort for negligence. In reasoning that was approved by the Court of Appeal (*ARB v IVF Hammersmith* [2018] EWCA Civ 2803; [2019] 2 W.L.R. 1094), Jay J held that a claim could not be brought for the substantial costs that the claimant said that he would incur in assisting to raise the child. Although the decisions of the House of Lords in *McFarlane v Tayside Health Board* [2000] 2 A.C. 59; [1999] 3 W.L.R. 1301 and *Rees v Darlington Memorial Hospital NHS Trust* [2003] UKHL 52; [2004] 1 A.C. 309 were concerned only with the law of torts and not with the law of contract, the foundation for the refusal of substantial damages in those cases must apply equally to contract. In contract in ARB, as in tort in those cases, the liability is based upon an assumption of responsibility to the claimant. The fundamental principle is the same. As Nicola Davies LJ said in the leading judgment in the Court of Appeal, it did not matter that the contract involved the claimant who paid for the services but that a claim for a tort need not, and could be brought if the services had been provided by the NHS (*ARB v IVF Hammersmith* [2018] EWCA Civ 2803; [2019] 2 W.L.R. 1094 at [37]).

PART 4A CONTRACT

CHAPTER 25

SALE OF GOODS

TABLE OF CONTENTS

I. BREACH BY SELLER

4. BREACH OF CONDITION OR WARRANTY AS TO QUALITY, FITNESS OR
    DESCRIPTION: GOODS ACCEPTED

(1) Normal measure

(b) Relevant and irrelevant prices in ascertaining the value of the goods as they are

Replace para.25-069 with:

How then should the position be resolved? It is submitted that Auld LJ's ap-   **25-069**
proach is to be preferred, according as it does with the reality of the situation. It is
difficult to see how Otton LJ can justify a different result depending upon whether
the goods are sold on in the same condition or after an anticipated modification, and
one suspects that were he presented with a situation similar to that in *Slater*,[305] he
would wish to decide the case as he decided *Bence Graphics*.[306] And surely the
answer to Scrutton LJ's attempted justification of the result in *Slater*,[307] on the

[77]

ground that the buyer might have bought substitute goods for the sub-contract is that, if the buyer, acting reasonably, had preferred not to foist the defective goods upon his sub-buyer but had supplied him with substitute goods and retained the defective ones, then the difference in value of the goods as they are and as they ought to have been does mark his real loss and, accordingly, the measure of his damages.[308] However, in *OMV Petrom SA v Glencore International AG*,[309] the Court of Appeal, without deciding, seemed to indicate a preference for the view of the Court of Appeal in *Slater v Hoyle & Smith*,[310] over that of the later Court of Appeal in *Bence Graphics v Fasson*.[311] The Court of Appeal in *OMV Petrom* observed that the reliance by Auld LJ in *Bence* on the Privy Council decision in *Wertheim v Chicoutimi Pulp Co*,[312] was upon a decision which Scrutton LJ thought was erroneous.[313] But, as we have seen above there is a simple explanation which answers the concerns that Scrutton LJ had about the decision in *Wertheim*.[314] In contrast, in *Euro-Asian Oil SA v Credit Suisse AG* [2018] EWCA Civ 1720; [2019] 1 All E.R. (Comm) 706 the damages for a failure to deliver a cargo of oil were limited to the loss from the sub-sale. The parties knew that the cargo of oil would be nominated to perform the sub-contract; there was no possibility that the cargo would be put to any other use. Simon LJ (with whom King LJ and Dame Elizabeth Gloster agreed) held that the prima facie rule in s.51(3), allowing recovery of the difference between market price and value of the goods provided, was displaced.

[305] [1920] 2 K.B. 11 CA.

[306] [1998] Q.B. 87 CA; [1997] 3 W.L.R. 205.

[307] [1920] 2 K.B. 11 CA.

[308] See similarly for delayed delivery para.25-042, above. The matter is further considered on a more general basis in Ch.9, above, at paras 9-171 and following.

[309] [2016] EWCA Civ 778; [2017] 3 All E.R. 157.

[310] [1920] 2 K.B. 11 CA.

[311] [1998] Q.B. 87 CA; [1997] 3 W.L.R. 205.

[312] [1911] A.C. 301.

[313] [2016] EWCA Civ 778; [2017] 3 All E.R. 157 at [45].

[314] See para.25-042, above.

CHAPTER 27

SALE OF LAND

TABLE OF CONTENTS

II. BREACH BY BUYER

(A) FAILURE TO ACCEPT

(2) CONSEQUENTIAL LOSSES

At the end of para.27-038, after "to the defendant.", add:

However, the costs of resale will also include any carrying costs, such as bridg- **27-038**
ing finance, which can naturally arise from the breach. Hence, in *Conway v Eze*
[2018] EWHC 29 (Ch) (appeal pending), five months of bridging finance until the
time of a likely resale was recoverable because it ought reasonably to have been

within the contemplation of the parties notwithstanding that the particular financial limitations of the vendor were not known: (at [165], [167]).

After para.27-038, add a new paragraph:

27-038A   An unusual circumstance where the usual consequential losses were not fully recovered due to a failure to mitigate arose in *Conway v Eze* [2018] EWHC 29 (Ch) (appeal pending). In that case, a buyer failed to complete a contract for the sale of land for £5 million. The land was resold for £4.2 million, which was found to be its true value. However, although the resale occurred shortly after the buyer's default, the date for completion of the resale was 15 months after the buyer's default, rather than the usual period of around two months. As a result of the cost of bridging finance this reduced the value of the purchase price, in real terms, to approximately £3.7 million. The trial judge, His Honour Judge Keyser QC, found that the buyer had established a failure by the vendor to mitigate when they knew that the market value of the property was £4.2 million. He concluded, not without speculation, that completion of another contract would have occurred within 5 months. This conclusion should be treated as turning upon the particular facts of the case. It should be unusual for a finding of a failure to mitigate to apply to a vendor who accepts the best available offer shortly after a purchaser's failure to complete particularly where the vendor is carrying substantial bridging finance and is anxious to sell.

CHAPTER 29

SALE OF SHARES AND LOAN OF STOCK

I.   BREACH BY SELLER

2.   OTHER BREACHES

After para.20-008, add a new paragraph:

In *Oversea-Chinese Banking Corp Ltd v ING Bank NV* [2019] EWHC 676   **29-008**
(Comm), the breach of a warranty as to quality was said to have arisen in an agreement between ING Bank and the defendant, OCBC. The agreement was for the sale of shares held by ING Bank in a target company. OCBC alleged that ING Bank had failed to record properly an exposure to Lehman Brothers Finance SA. The target company later settled a claim based on that exposure. OCBC alleged that it would have obtained an indemnity against that exposure but for the negligent accounting. Although finding that OCBC did not prove any breach and also that it failed to prove that an indemnity would have been sought and obtained by it, the trial judge concluded that damages for breach of a warranty as to quality are limited to the diminution in the value of the shares at the time of purchase, rather than a hypothetical indemnity that would have been obtained. After referring to the paragraph above, and the cases discussed there, the primary judge concluded that the loss from the failure to obtain an indemnity could not be recovered as damages (at [40]). Strictly, however, none of the cases in para.20-008 addressed the availability of a loss arising from the failure to obtain an indemnity. However, the reason why the judge was correct to refuse recovery for the failure to obtain an indemnity was because it was not an additional loss. If the accounting treatment had been negligent and if the shares were consequently worth less than what was paid for them at the time of purchase as a result, then a reasonable purchaser in OCBC's position would have been entitled to recover that loss. For OCBC also to recover the amount of a claim on an indemnity that it failed to obtain would mean that it would be compensated for both the normal loss based on the reduced value of the shares due to the prospect of that exposure as well as the later loss when the same exposure arose.

CONSTRUCTION CONTRACTS

I.   Breach By Builder

1.   Failure to Build at all or in Part

(1)   Normal measure

Replace footnote 11 with:

[11] Or that part of the contract price, if any, remaining unpaid. See *Byrne v Rose* [2019] NZHC 273 at **31-004**
[209] approving this passage.

CHAPTER 32

CONTRACTS OF CARRIAGE

II. BREACH BY CARGO OWNER

1. FAILURE TO SUPPLY CARGO

(1) Normal measure

(c) Normal measure not always recoverable to end of contractual period

Replace para.32-074 with:

Where there is breach of a charterparty by its wrongful cancellation by the **32-074**
charterers, the normal damages measure of charter rate of freight less market rate
may not be available for the full remaining contractual period in some circumstances if the charterer could have rightfully cancelled the contract. As the law presently stands, whether the damages are available depends upon whether the repudia-
tion was an anticipatory breach or not. This is a neat and principled distinction but,
as we saw in Ch.10, it is not one that aligns perfectly with cases in other areas. The
best illustration is *Classic Maritime Inc v Limbungan Makmur Sdn Bhd* [2019]
EWCA Civ 1102; [2019] 2 All E.R. (Comm) 592. In that case, the charterer failed

to provide cargoes to the ship owner. The charterer later argued that it could not be liable for substantial damages for failure to be ready and willing to perform because a burst dam would have excused performance. The Court of Appeal held that the charterer's duty was to deliver and it breached that duty. It did not matter whether it might have been excused from being ready and willing to perform. The circumstance of anticipatory breach is different because the duty breached in that case is a duty to be ready and willing to perform. The value of that right might be negligible if performance was never going to be received for reasons other than breach (such as the burst dam). Hence, damages will be nominal after the point of termination for anticipatory breach if the charterers would have become entitled rightfully to cancel the charterparty, and would have done so, at a point in time later than the wrongful cancellation. In *Maredelanto Compania Naviera SA v Bergbau-Handel GmbH, The Mihalis Angelos* [1971] 1 Q.B. 164 CA; [1970] 3 W.L.R. 601, breach came even before performance by the charterers was due to commence, the wrongful cancellation having been an anticipatory breach accepted by the shipowners, and only nominal damages were awarded since rightful cancellation would have immediately and inevitably followed. So too where the charterers' right to cancel was anticipated as a near certainty in *BS&N Ltd v Mikado Shipping Ltd (The Seaflower)* [2000] 2 All E.R. (Comm) 169; [2000] 2 Lloyd's Rep. 37, the damages only extended to the time that rightful cancellation would have happened. More difficulty was encountered in *Golden Strait Corp v Nippon Yusen Kubishika Kaisha (The Golden Victory)* [2007] UKHL 12; [2007] 2 A.C. 353, where it was not known at the time of wrongful cancellation that the possibility of rightful cancellation would arise in the future. The great question therefore was whether or not, in assessing the shipowners' damages, the court could regard and take into account events after the wrongful cancellation, being events which gave the charterers a right to cancel. On this there was a sharp division of view, three of their Lordships deciding in the charterers' favour, two in the shipowners'.

Chapter 34

CONTRACTS FOR PROFESSIONAL AND OTHER SERVICES

Table of Contents

II Breach by the Party Rendering the Services

(B) Particular Categories

1. Solicitors

(1) Pecuniary loss

(b) Negligence in the acquisition of property by purchase

(ii) Consequential losses

After the first sentence, add:

An initial question in relation to recovery of consequential losses may be whether **34-016**
those losses could be said to be losses for which the solicitors had assumed
responsibility. In some cases, the losses will be beyond that about which the solicitors assumed responsibility. This argument was made in *Main v Giambrone* [2017]
EWCA Civ 1193; [2018] P.N.L.R. 2, where a law firm advised English and Irish
claimants that they would be protected by bank loan guarantees when buying Italian property off the plan. The firm received and then paid out the claimant's deposits
without guarantees being in place. But the deposits were lost after it was discovered
that the whole transaction was a scam and a money laundering scheme by the mafia.

Nevertheless, the firm, with its Italian lawyers, were found to have assumed responsibility for the transaction because they guided the "whole decision making process" (at [82]).

(f) Negligent conduct of litigation

After para.34-036, add a new paragraph:

34-036A   In exceptional circumstances, there is also the possibility of damages for non-pecuniary loss caused by the negligence of solicitors. As explained in Ch.5, the award of non-pecuniary loss should require a focus upon the extent to which the parties contemplated that psychological benefits were an object of the contract. Exceptionally, non-pecuniary loss might be recoverable where a substantial purpose of the solicitor's retainer is to obtain peace of mind. Hence, in *Shaw v Leigh Day (A Firm)* [2017] EWHC 825 (QB); [2017] P.N.L.R. 26, a claim for damages for mental distress was permitted to go to trial where it was arguable that the known objective of a legal retainer to represent the claimant at an inquest into her father's death was to obtain peace of mind (at [25], [29]).

2.   SURVEYORS AND VALUERS

There will be a change of title:

34-049   In the next mainwork this heading will be changed to "Surveyors, Valuers, and Progress Monitors".

(1)   Purchasers of property negligently surveyed or valued

(a)   Pecuniary loss: normal measure

At the end of para.34-055, after "at market value.", add:

34-055   Of course, if the parties, for tactical reasons, choose to litigate the case without providing any evidence that could be sufficient even to estimate the market valuation, then a judge can be justified in using the cost of repairs as evidence of the difference in price. As Birss J observed in *Moore v National Westminster Bank* [2018] EWHC 1805 (TCC); [2018] B.L.R. 586, this tactic backfired when the defendant adduced no evidence of value and made no submissions about any value of the property other than a risible sum that was not supported by the evidence. The claimant's damages against the lender who negligently failed to provide a report were upheld in the amount of £115,000, being the repair costs, although the price of the entire property was only £135,000.

(2)   Mortgagees of property negligently surveyed or valued

(c)   Consequential losses: what is generally irrecoverable

(i)   Losses from fall in market

Replace footnote 356 with:

34-074   356 [2017] UKSC 21; [2017] 2 W.L.R. 1029 at [40]–[41]. See also *Lloyds Bank Plc v McBains Cooper Consulting Ltd* [2018] EWCA Civ 452; [2018] 1 B.C.L.C. 609 at [33].

After the third sub-section, add a new sub-section:

(4)   Mortgagees and lenders negligently advised by Progress Monitors

Lloyds Bank Plc v McBains Cooper Consulting Ltd [2018] EWCA Civ 452; **34-082A**
[2018] 1 B.C.L.C. 609 is an instance of negligence by a progress monitor engaged
by a bank to report about the progress of a building contract and to make recom-
mendations about interim payments. The progress monitor failed to inform the bank
that the bank was being asked to pay for work done outside the terms of the loan
facility. The Court of Appeal held, following *Hughes-Holland v BPE Solicitors*
[2017] UKSC 21; [2017] 2 W.L.R. 1029 at [39], that it did not matter whether the
negligence was characterised as negligently advising the bank to make the payment or as negligently failing to provide the bank with information that the payment sought was outside the terms of the loan facility. In that case, the damages to
which the bank was entitled were limited to the sums paid out for that work because
but for the negligence the bank would still have continued with the loss-making
contract.

3.   Accountants

After para.34-083, add a new paragraph:

Ultimately, as with lawyers, the scope of liability for accountants for negligent **34-083A**
advice will depend upon the subject matter for which the accountants have assumed responsibility. Although the labels of "advice" and "information" are
descriptively inadequate, courts have focused upon whether the task performed by
the accountants was one of "advice" in the sense that responsibility was assumed
for the consequences of entry into the transaction, or "information" where the
information provider does not take responsibility for the decision to enter the
transaction. In *Manchester Building Society v Grant Thornton UK LLP* [2019]
EWCA Civ 40; [2019] 1 W.L.R. 4610, the negligence by the respondent accountants in their accounting treatment of long-term interest rate swaps entered by the
building society did not lead to their liability for all of the consequences of the
transaction when the decision to enter the swaps was based upon a number of commercial considerations entirely separate from the accounting advice. Hamblen LJ,
with whom Males LJ and Dame Elizabeth Gloster agreed, repeated the trial judge's
observation that it would be "a striking conclusion to reach that an accountant who
advises a client as to the manner in which its business activities may be treated in
its accounts has assumed responsibility for the financial consequences of those business activities" (at [99]).

PART 4B TORT

CHAPTER 39

TORTS AFFECTING LAND

TABLE OF CONTENTS

I. DAMAGE

1. NORMAL MEASURE

(1) In general

To the end of the paragraph, after "allowed damages accordingly.", add:

However, in *Hyde v Simple Skips Ltd* [2017] EWHC 3087 (QB), Justine **39-013** Thornton QC, sitting as a Deputy High Court Judge, held that an expensive reinstatement and remediation of waste was reasonable where the claimant had received planning permission subject to approval of a remediation scheme for the site, and the claimant had been subject to an Environment Agency notice and actions concerning removal of the waste.

II. Occupation and User

3. Consequential Losses

Replace para.39-068 with:

39-068   In addition, claims for non-pecuniary loss would seem to be in order; to be dispossessed of one's property, or to have its use interfered with, may well cause inconvenience, discomfort and distress. However, such claims will generally give rise to an entitlement to aggravated damages since they will stem from culpable and unattractive conduct of the defendant; such damages are dealt with later.[363] At this point, it suffices to mention the usual award of general damages that is made in cases of this nature. In *Smith v Khan* [2018] EWCA Civ 1137; [2018] H.L.R. 31, the Court of Appeal upheld the conclusion of Judge Owen that the range of awards of general damages for trespass are between £100 and £300 per night. As Patten LJ (with whom Henderson and Newey LJJ agreed) explained, the award must compensate the tenant for (i) the letting value of the property of which he or she has been deprived, and (ii) the anxiety, inconvenience and mental stress involved in the loss of what was the tenant's home (at [45]). In that case, the eviction of the claimant, who was the wife of the absent tenant and therefore entitled to be treated as a tenant under s.30(4)(b) of the Family Law Act 1996, occurred in circumstances where the property was the family home and the eviction was without consent and without notice to the wife. The period of the trespass for which damages could be awarded was the entire period of unlawful occupation by the landlord; the damages were not to be reduced by a hypothetical consideration of when the landlord would lawfully have been able to evict the claimant (at [39]). This conclusion is correct in relation to the "user" damages and distress damages, but it might be doubted in relation to other consequential damages. The eviction led to an award of £9,880. This was comprised of a daily amount of £130. Although this seems to be at the lower end of the scale, the reason may be the longer period for which the award applied. If the trespass had been only a few days, it is likely that the daily rate would be considerably higher, reflecting the increased anxiety and stress consequent upon the initial trespass.

[363] See para.39-072, below.

CHAPTER 40

TORTS CAUSING PERSONAL INJURY

TABLE OF CONTENTS

Replace para.40-003 with:

A preliminary question of fact in every personal injury case is whether action-   **40-003**
able damage has been suffered. A physical injury requires a non-negligible impairment of a person's health, which could be manifest or hidden. In other words, the
person must be "appreciably worse off in respect of his 'health or capability'"
(*Dryden v Johnson Matthey Plc* [2018] UKSC 18; [2018] 2 W.L.R. 1109 at [27]).
In *Dryden v Johnson Matthey Plc*, the respondent company negligently failed to
ensure that its factories were properly cleaned. The claimants were exposed to
platinum salts and developed platinum salt sensitisation involving the presence of
an antibody in their systems. Although that condition was asymptomatic, it was not
benign. The sensitivity meant that if the person was further exposed to platinum
salts he or she would develop an allergic reaction involving physical symptoms. The
expert evidence was that since platinum salts are not encountered in everyday life,
the effect of sensitisation is only that the person cannot work in a job that involves
the potential for further exposure. In this respect, platinum sensitisation is different from pleural plaques, considered in *Rothwell v Chemical and Insulating Co Ltd*
[2007] UKHL 39; [2008] 1 A.C. 281, which do not develop into any further condition and do not involve any restrictions on the person.

Lady Black JSC (with whom Lady Hale PSC, Lords Wilson, Reed and Lloyd-
Jones JJSC agreed) followed the approach in *Cartledge v E Jopling & Sons Ltd*
[1963] A.C. 758; [1963] 2 W.L.R. 210 which held that pneumoconiosis, which dam-
aged lung tissue and reduced its efficiency, was an actionable injury despite the fact
that, in Lord Pearce's words, the person has "no knowledge of the secret onset of
pneumoconiosis and suffers no present inconvenience from it". In contrast, *Rothwell
v Chemical and Insulating Co Ltd* [2007] UKHL 39; [2008] 1 A.C. 281 was
distinguished because pleural plaques were not merely symptomless; they also had
no effect on a person's health (at [47]). The platinum sensitisation was a bodily

change that left the claimants appreciably worse off by being unable to work in a job that was part of their everyday life (at [39]–[40]).

I. FORMS OF AWARD AND OF COMPENSATION

1. INTERIM AWARDS

Replace para.40-006 with:

40-006 The availability of interim payments can help with the problem of the uncertainty of the future because the need to proceed with great speed to the end of the litigation is reduced. This is particularly true where advantage is taken, where appropriate, of splitting the claim into two parts, so that the issue of liability is decided first and the assessment of damages is arrived at later, with provision for the awarding at the hearing on liability of interim payments on account of the final award; this helps to deal with perhaps the most frequent cause of a damages award turning out to be wrongly based, namely a substantial change in the claimant's condition, which in the nature of things is most likely to occur within the first years after the injury. Interim payments may also be awarded where liability is admitted[20] and where the court is satisfied that at trial the claimant would obtain judgment for substantial damages.[21] No more than a reasonable proportion of the likely amount of the final judgment should be ordered.[22] Nevertheless, a reasonable proportion may well be a high proportion, even 90% (*TTT v Hospital NHS Trust* [2011] EWHC 3917 (QB)) of the loss incurred, although possibly limited to the loss at the time of payment (*Folkes v General Assurances* [2019] EWHC 801 (QB) at [26]), especially if the estimate is conservative so that there is no risk of overpayment: see *Folkes v General Assurances* [2019] EWHC 801 (QB) at [64]–[65].

[20] CPR r.25.7(1)(a).

[21] CPR r.25.7(1)(c). Where with liability admitted the court is satisfied that substantial damages will be awarded but it is currently difficult to conclude accurately what sum will be recovered, the assessment must be carried out on a conservative basis and the risk of overpayment avoided: *AS v West Suffolk Hospital Trust* unreported 1 May 2015.

[22] CPR r.25.7(4); as to the interpretation of this see *Spillman v Bradfield Riding Centre* [2007] EWHC 89 (QB). Pt IV of the Law Commission's Report on *Structured Settlements and Interim and Provisional Damages* (Law Com. No.224 (1994)) has a valuable discussion of the various issues concerning interim payments. The practice which developed has had to be modified to accommodate the periodical payments regime along the lines set out by the Court of Appeal in *Eeles v Cobham Hire Services Ltd* [2009] EWCA Civ 204; [2010] 1 W.L.R. 409 CA.

3. PERIODICAL PAYMENTS AWARDS

(2) Matters in issue

(d) Security of continuity of awards

After para.40-029, add a new paragraph:

40-029A The requirement for payments to be reasonably secure is an assessment that is expressed in the present tense. When events occur that give rise to uncertainty then the question should always be whether the uncertainty causes the court to conclude that, at the present time, continuity of payment is not reasonably secure. For instance, in *Young v Bennett* [2018] EWHC 3555 (QB) a question was whether the court was satisfied that continuity of payment of periodical payments was reasonably secure despite the future uncertainty of the "Brexit" process by which the

United Kingdom would exit from the European Union. Master McCloud held that although it was unclear whether the applicability of the financial services compensation scheme would be affected if Brexit occurred, the periodical payments were presently reasonably secure (at [22]).

IV. LOSS OF EARNING CAPACITY AND RELATED BENEFITS

To the end of the paragraph, add:

This also explains why in *Head v The Culver Heating Co Ltd* [2019] EWHC **40-062**
1217 (QB), her Honour Judge Melissa Clarke was correct to hold that the claimant's earnings of more than £4 million during the lost years were irrecoverable because those earnings comprised dividends from capital that the claimant already owned at the time of death.

After para.40-062, add a new paragraph:

In *Pickett v British Rail Engineering Ltd* [1980] A.C. 136 at 148, Lord **40-062A**
Wilberforce spoke of the claim by a living person for loss of earnings during the lost years. That prompted his concern to address the objection that nothing is of value to a person who is not alive to enjoy it. His answer to that objection was that what was lost was the "existing capability to earn well for 14 years". He had been "deprived of his ability to earn". That capability was of value to him because even if the income could not be used it could be left to dependants or causes that the claimant supported (at 149). Lord Wilberforce relied in part upon the reasoning of principle of the great Australian judge, Windeyer J, in the High Court of Australia in *Skelton v Collins* (1966) 115 C.L.R. 94 at 129, see [1980] A.C. 136 at 150–151. In that case, Windeyer J had described the loss as a loss of "earning capacity", not a loss of earnings. This characterisation was critical in the decision of the High Court of Australia in *Amaca Pty Ltd v Latz* [2018] HCA 22; [2018] 92 A.L.J.R. 579 at [89], where the majority said that the loss "has been described as a capital asset - the capacity to earn money from the use of personal skills".

(A) GENERAL METHOD OF ASSESSMENT

Replace the first sentence of the paragraph with:

The well known principle to calculate loss of future earnings was explained by **40-066**
Lord Lloyd-Jones giving the advice of the Privy Council in *Cadet's Car Rentals v Pinder* [2019] UKPC 4 at [14].

(B) CALCULATION OF THE MULTIPLICAND AND OF THE MULTIPLIER

3. ADJUSTMENTS FOR VARIATION IN ANNUAL EARNINGS LOSS

(2) Handicap in the labour market: then and now

(a) The introduction of Smith v Manchester awards

In para.40-098, after "competing in the labour market.", add:

And in *Foreman v Williams* [2017] EWHC 3370 (QB) at [47] an award of **40-098**
£23,000 was made where the claimant remained in his employment but there was only a "real risk" that he might lose his job "at some point in the future" and then find it harder to obtain a new job.

5. Adjustments Where Life Expectancy is Cut Down by the Injury

(2) The question of the lost years

Replace para.40-109 with:

40-109   In 1962 in *Oliver v Ashman*,[467] the Court of Appeal came down in favour of making the assessment on the post-injury life expectancy, thereby resolving for a period the uncertainty which had by then been generated by conflicting decisions of courts of first instance.[468] In so deciding, the Court of Appeal regarded the matter as concluded for itself by the decision in *Benham v Gambling*,[469] and by the remarks of Viscount Simon who delivered a speech with which all the other Law Lords concurred.[470] That case, however, was concerned with the awarding of damages for loss of expectation of life to the estate of a person fatally injured[471] and the House of Lords in *Pickett v British Rail Engineering*,[472] concluded that *Benham* "was no authority compelling the decision in *Oliver v Ashman*"[473] because Viscount Simon

"did not have in mind a claim by a living person for earnings during the lost years".[474]

Authority therefore not standing in its way, the House proceeded to overrule[475]*Oliver v Ashman*.[476] While, in choosing to base the damages upon the post-injury life expectancy, *Oliver v Ashman* may have avoided an award to the claimant of "wages in heaven" and may appear consequently to have faithfully followed the compensatory principle which underlies the whole law of damages, the decision was now seen as a short-sighted one because it ignored the fact that it left no moneys available to the claimant out of which to make provision after his death for his dependants, who are generally assumed to be precluded by the claimant's successful action from themselves making any claim under the Fatal Accidents Act. It had indeed been urged upon their Lordships that, the real loss being to the victim's dependants, the right way to compensate them was to change the law by statute to enable the dependants to recover their loss independently of any action by the victim. This approach was also urged in all earlier editions of this work, although it was felt that it could be achieved within the existing framework and therefore without the need for legislation.[477] Since there was no Fatal Accidents Act claim in *Pickett v British Rail Engineering Ltd* [1980] A.C. 136; [1978] 3 W.L.R. 955, Lord Wilberforce proceeded on the assumption that no dependants' claim could follow upon the injured party's claim [1980] A.C. 136 at 146. That assumption thus

"provides a basis, in logic and justice, for allowing the victim to recover for earnings lost during his lost years".

Yet 25 years later we find, again in the House of Lords, Lord Phillips had this to say in *Gregg v Scott* [2005] UKHL 2; [2005] 2 A.C. 176 at [182]:

"It would be much better if the claimant had no right to recover for such loss of earnings and the dependants' right to claim under s.1(1) of the Fatal Accidents Act 1976 subsisted despite the claimant's recovery of damages for his injury. I am not persuaded that this result could not be achieved by a purposive construction of that section."

This concern is based upon a misunderstanding of the basis for the award of damages for loss of earning capacity. The loss of earning capacity is not the same as a loss of wages during the lost years. It is an immediate and existing loss to the living claimant. As the majority of the High Court of Australia said in *Amaca Pty Ltd v Latz* [2018] HCA 22; [2018] 92 A.L.J.R. 579 at [89], it "has been described as a capital asset - the capacity to earn money from the use of personal skills".

[467] [1962] 2 Q.B. 210 CA; [1961] 3 W.L.R. 669.

[468] In *Harris v Brights Asphalt Contractors* [1953] 1 Q.B. 617; [1953] 1 W.L.R. 341 damages had been awarded on the post-injury life expectancy, but in *Pope v Murphy* [1961] 1 Q.B. 222; [1960] 2 W.L.R. 861 and at first instance in *Oliver v Ashman* [1961] 1 Q.B. 337; [1960] 3 W.L.R. 924 itself, the awards were based on the pre-injury life expectancy.

[469] [1941] A.C. 157; [1941] 1 All E.R. 7.

[470] See [1962] 2 Q.B. 210 CA at 229, 238, 244.

[471] See para.41-133, below.

[472] [1980] A.C. 136; [1978] 3 W.L.R. 955.

[473] [1980] A.C. 136 at 148E, per Lord Wilberforce.

[474] [1980] A.C. 136 at 148E.

[475] Lord Russell dissenting.

[476] [1962] 2 Q.B. 210 CA; [1961] 3 W.L.R. 669.

[477] As explained at para.41-008, below.

Replace para.40-110 with:

Cases have rarely considered claims for pecuniary losses suffered in the lost years **40-110** that do not arise from a loss of earning capacity. An obvious extension is the pension benefits that would be payable during the lost years either as part of the loss of earning capacity or based on earnings before the expected death: see *Amaca Pty Ltd v Latz* [2018] HCA 22; [2018] 92 A.L.J.R. 579. In *Gammell v Wilson* [1982] A.C. 27 at 77, Lord Scarman (with whom Lord Fraser agreed) contemplated that an annuity that ceased upon death could be recovered as part of the cause of action that vested before death. Just as the loss of earning capacity is described as the loss of the value of a "capital asset" so too is the loss of value of an annuity arising from the lost years. On the other hand, some cases have gone further to allow for the recovery of losses during the lost years that are not existing rights but merely lost chances. In *Adsett v West* [1983] Q.B. 826; [1983] 3 W.L.R. 437 a lost years claim was held to encompass recovery for the lost prospect of an inheritance. That loss of chance recovery was rejected by the minority judges, and carefully avoided by the majority judges, in the High Court of Australia in *Amaca Pty Ltd v Latz* [2018] HCA 22; [2018] 92 A.L.J.R. 579 at [115].

V. MEDICAL AND RELATED EXPENSES

(A) EXPENSES INCLUDED

1. MEDICAL EXPENSES

(1) In general

Replace para.40-184 with:

However, *Briody* was distinguished in *XX v Whittington Hospital NHS Trust* **40-184** [2018] EWCA Civ 2832; [2019] 3 W.L.R. 107. Changes in legislation in 2008 had removed the unlawful nature of surrogacy and it was no longer contrary to public policy to enter into non-profit surrogacy arrangements. Both the trial judge and the Court of Appeal held that the claimant could recover the costs of a United Kingdom surrogacy for two children using the claimant's own eggs because on the balance of probabilities that surrogacy would achieve two live births. However, despite the strong obiter dicta of Hale LJ in *Briody* doubting whether a claim for surrogacy is restorative of the loss of a woman's ability to have her own child, the Court of Appeal disagreed with the trial judge and held that damages could also be recovered for "donor egg" surrogacy conducted in the United States or the United Kingdom. Damages are never perfectly restorative of an injury. Their aim is to do the best that can be done to restore. Further, as the Court of Appeal said, a distinction between "own egg" surrogacy and "donor egg" surrogacy is artificial (at [94], [105], [106]).

(2) Medical treatment and care provided privately and provided by the National Health Service or by local authorities

(b) Private care and local authority care

After para.40-192, add a new paragraph:

40-192A   The choice by a claimant of self-funding is not, however, irrevocable. In *R. (Tinsley) v Manchester City Council* [2018] Q.B. 767 CA; [2018] 2 W.L.R. 973, the Court of Appeal considered a case where a claimant was awarded damages that included a component for costs of care on the basis that his desired requirements, as well as reasonable requirements, would not be met by his local authority. Subsequently, however, after mismanagement of the judgment funds on his behalf, the claimant sought to rely upon s.117 of the Mental Health Act 1983 as creating an obligation for the local authority to care for him. That obligation arose where the person had been released from detention in a mental health facility. In *R. v Manchester City Council; ex Parte Stennett* [2002] UKHL 34; [2002] 2 A.C. 1127 the House of Lords had held that after-care services under s.117 could not be the subject of a charge. The local authority sought to deny liability to provide care on the basis that damages had been awarded for that purpose. Longmore LJ (with whom the Master of the Rolls and Irwin LJ agreed) rejected this submission.

2.   Related Expenses

(5)   Special accommodation expenses

To the end of the paragraph, add:

40-207   However, William Davis J considered himself bound by *Roberts v Johnstone*. An appeal was subsequently compromised on terms that the defendant pay a substantial proportion of the capital costs: see *LP v Wye Valley NHS Trust* [2018] EWHC 3039 (QB) at [35]. Likewise, Lambert J in *Swift v Carpenter* [2018] EWHC 2060 (QB) treated *Roberts v Johnstone* as binding upon her. An appeal from that decision is pending.

Replace the first sentence of the paragraph with:

40-208   It is increasingly recognised that it is high time that the *Roberts v Johnstone* problem was tackled and a fair and proper solution found and adopted: *Porter v Barts Health NHS Trust* [2017] EWHC 3205 (QB) at [27]–[28].

After para.40-208, add a new paragraph:

40-208A   The solution adopted in *LP v Wye Valley NHS Trust* [2018] EWHC 3039 (QB) was effectively to treat *Roberts v Johnstone* as inapplicable to circumstances involving negative discount rates. This approach is arbitrary but it is at least consistent with the principle that just as a discount rate that would award more than the capital value must be erroneous, to refuse any recovery for the capital cost of accommodation must also be erroneous because it is effectively to deny the fundamental principle that compensation be given for reasonable, proven losses caused by wrongdoing. Instead, in that case a rate of 1.3% was adopted, being the conservative rate of return if investing over 30 years. But there remains, however, the further anomaly that unless *Roberts v Johnstone* were to be ignored entirely then the discount rate of -0.75% would lead to a larger award than a discount rate of 0.1%. The inequities arising from such comparisons might only be resolvable by instead adopting *Roberts v Johnstone* with the recognition of an alternative, in cases where the fundamental principle of compensation would be violated of the full purchase price but with a charge on the purchased property in favour of the defendant realisable on the claimant's death: *Oxborrow v West Sussex Hospitals NHS Trust* [2012] EWHC 1010 (QB); [2012] Med. L.R. 297 at [47].

VI. NON-PECUNIARY DAMAGE

2. HEADS OF NON-PECUNIARY DAMAGE

After para.40-254, add a new paragraph:

It has been observed that the combination of awards for pain and suffering and loss of amenity can limit the utility of comparisons: *Gallardo v Imperial College Healthcare NHS Trust* [2017] EWHC 3147 (QB); [2018] P.I.Q.R. P6 at [108]. However, sometimes this award can comprise almost the entirety of the damages. An example is the decision of His Honour Judge Peter Hughes QC sitting as a High Court judge in *Gallardo v Imperial College Healthcare NHS Trust* [2017] EWHC 3147 (QB); [2018] P.I.Q.R. P6. In that case, the claimant underwent major abdominal surgery for the removal of a tumour in 2001. Due to the negligence of the defendant he was not informed that the tumour was malignant and might return. The tumour returned. It would have been diagnosed and then treated in 2007 if the claimant had been properly advised but instead it was not treated for a further four years. An award of pain, suffering and loss of amenity was made of £27,500. This was for (i) the distress of being told the true position nine years late; (ii) the consequent need for more complex surgery, difficulty in recovery, and possible future complications; and (iii) years of additional pain and suffering following the failure to detect the recurrence and operate upon it and anxiety in trying to discover the true nature of the condition. **40-254A**

(4) Other possible heads of loss

(i) Loss of congenial employment

Replace para.40-265 with:

In quite recent years it has become a feature of personal injury cases where the claimant is no longer able to continue in his former employment to make a separate award under the rubric "loss of congenial employment". One can trace the idea as far back as *Hale v London Underground*,[1253] where it was already being said, at first instance, that loss of congenial employment was "now well recognised ... [as] a separate head of damage"[1254] though no authority for this was cited. Certainly, in the early years of this century this head of damage was being recognised by the Court of Appeal, both in *Willbye v Gibbons*,[1255] and in *Chase International Express Ltd v McRae*.[1256] Awards continue to this day at first instance, and in relation to a whole variety of employments. In *Dudney v Guaranteed Asphalt Ltd*,[1257] a roofer **40-265** was awarded £5,000, an amount said to be at the bottom of the range[1258]; in *Evans v Virgin Atlantic Airways*,[1259] a beauty therapist was held to merit what was said to be a relatively high award,[1260] coming out at £10,000; and in *Davison v Leach*,[1261]*Dudney* and *Evans* were followed so as to £6,500 to an equity sales trader working in the financial sector. And in *Inglis v Ministry of Defence* [2019] EWHC 1153 (QB), the court awarded £8,000 for the loss of enjoyment of seven years of military service, referring to similar cases with different lengths of employment lost where the awards for this head of damages were, adjusted for inflation, of £14,800 and £11,000: see *Brown v Ministry of Defence* [2006] EWCA Civ 546; [2006] P.I.Q.R. Q9; *Murphy v Ministry of Defence* [2016] EWHC 3 (QB). In contrast, where the claimant had not yet established herself in her career, and would be able to return to the career within two years, no award was made under this head: *Zeromska-Smith v United Lincolnshire Hospitals NHS Trust* [2019] EWHC 980 (QB) at [111]–[112]. The two earlier Court of Appeal decisions are instructive. In *Willbye* the first instance award of £15,000 on account of loss of congenial employment was reduced to £5,000, Kennedy LJ saying that it was "important to keep this head of damages in proportion".[1262] In *Chase* the trial judge's award of £2,000 was set aside because the Court of Appeal did not regard the claimant, who worked as a motor cycle courier, as having provided enough evidence to indicate that he enjoyed riding his motor cycle and found his work as a motor cycle courier extremely satisfying. Significantly Kennedy LJ said[1263]:

> "The award can only be made to compensate a claimant for the loss of congenial employment, as the head of damages indicates. Any award for the interference with the satisfaction which a claimant gets, for example, out of the use of a motor cycle in his ordinary social life has to be compensated for under the head of pain, suffering and loss of amenities."

Yet why should there be a difference in the way of regarding the damages awarded between the joy of work and the joy of play? The professional motor cyclist seems to be no different from the professional violinist whose deprivation of the enjoyment of playing has often been regarded as compensable by way of loss of amenities. Nevertheless the courts are continuing to regard loss of congenial employment as a different category of non-pecuniary loss from loss of amenities. Nevertheless, a distinction must be drawn between enjoyment of work and simply being unable to perform the work in exactly the same way. Hence, in *Foreman v Williams* [2017] EWHC 3370 (QB) at [45] it was conceded by the claimant, and accepted by the trial judge, that it is not enough that a claimant, who remains in current employment, cannot undertake his job in exactly the same way as he did in the past.

[1253] [1993] P.I.Q.R. Q30.

[1254] [1993] P.I.Q.R. Q30 at 39.

[1255] [2003] EWCA Civ 372; [2004] P.I.Q.R. P15.

[1256] [2003] EWCA Civ 505; [2004] P.I.Q.R. P21.

[1257] [2013] EWHC 2515 (QB).

[1258] [2003] EWCA Civ 372; [2004] P.I.Q.R. P15 at [28]. In *Ward v Allies & Morrison Architects* Unreported, £5,000 was again awarded and to a young woman who had not yet started on her chosen career. The award was not challenged in the Court of Appeal: [2012] EWCA Civ 1287; [2013] P.I.Q.R. Q1 at [2].

[1259] [2011] EWHC 1805 (QB).

[1260] [2011] EWHC 1805 (QB) at [30].

[1261] [2013] EWHC 3092 (QB).

[1262] [2003] EWCA Civ 372; [2004] P.I.Q.R. P15 at [11].

[1263] [2003] EWCA Civ 505; [2004] P.I.Q.R. P15 at [22].

VII.   ENVOI: THE PARTICULAR CASE OF CLAIMS BY PARENTS ARISING OUT OF THE BIRTH OF THEIR CHILDREN

1.   SETTING THE SCENE

Replace footnote 1322 with:

[1322] Occasionally the claim may not be on account of having a child but on account of the failure to have   **40-282**
a child. See above at para.40-184 and especially the decision in *XX v Whittington Hospital NHS Trust*
[2018] EWCA Civ 2832; [2019] 3 W.L.R. 107.

4.   THE NEW THINKING EXTENDED: REES V DARLINGTON MEMORIAL HOSPITAL NHS TRUST

(2)   The invention of a conventional award

After para.40-293, add a new paragraph:

The confinement of damages to a conventional sum will occur whether the claim   **40-293A**
is brought in the law of torts or for breach of contract. In *ARB v IVF Hammersmith Ltd* [2017] EWHC 2438 (QB); [2018] 2 W.L.R. 1223, a father and mother
had IVF treatment at the defendant clinic. A child was born and spare embryos
remained frozen. After the relationship between the mother and father broke down
irretrievably, the mother forged the father's signature on a form that requested
consent for the embryos to be thawed. She was successful in having another child.
The father claimed against the clinic for breach of contract and sought damages for
the costs he would incur in bringing up the child including private education, a gap
year, university abroad, a generous wedding, refurbishing a bedroom. The clinic
sought indemnity from the mother on the basis of deceit. At first instance, Jay J held
that the clinic had breached an implied contractual duty to take care. As he
observed, the House of Lords in *McFarlane v Tayside Health Board* [2000] 2 A.C.
59; [1999] 3 W.L.R. 1301 and *Rees v Darlington Memorial Hospital NHS Trust*
[2003] UKHL 52; [2004] 1 A.C. 309 were concerned only with the law of torts and
not with the law of contract. Some of the rationales for refusing substantial damages as a matter of policy, such as the burden on the NHS and the issues of fair-
ness, justice and reasonableness in the tortious consideration of duty did not apply
in relation to breach of contract and, in *McFarlane*, Lords Slynn and Steyn had left
open the possibility that the result might be different for a breach of contract.
However, as Jay J correctly explained, the "universal statements of principle" in the
tort section of the 19th edition of this book (at [304]), must equally apply to breach
of contract. This conclusion was endorsed by the Court of Appeal. In the leading
judgment in the Court of Appeal, Nicola Davies LJ said that there should not be a
difference between a claimant who paid for the services and had a claim in contract
and a claimant who relied upon the NHS and had a claim in tort (*ARB v IVF Hammersmith* [2018] EWCA Civ 2803; [2018] 2 W.L.R. 1223 at [37]). The same result
from the law of torts applies also to contract due to this incongruity which would
arise from treating the same underlying right differently. The basis of the tortious
claim and the contract claim are identical: they both rest upon an assumption of
responsibility to take care.

5. The Position Today

(1) Extra costs of care of the disabled child: the still uncertain position

(b) Where there has been a failure to warn of disability

After para.40-297, add a new paragraph:

40-297A The most recent case involving a failure to warn of child's disability is *Khan v Meadows* [2019] EWCA Civ 152; [2019] 4 W.L.R 26. In that case, the pregnant claimant consulted the defendant doctor about the risk that her child would be born with haemophilia. The claimant was negligently, and incorrectly, advised that she was not a carrier. She chose not to terminate her pregnancy, which she otherwise would have done. Her child was born with haemophilia and, also, the unrelated condition of autism. It was admitted that the additional costs of haemophilia were recoverable but the Court of Appeal held that the additional costs of autism could not be recovered because they were outside the scope of the doctor's duty to warn. The risk of autism had not been increased by the doctor's negligence. *Chester v Afshar* [2004] UKHL 41; [2005] 1 A.C. 134 was distinguished because the misfortune in that case was the very misfortune against which the doctor had a duty to warn.

CHAPTER 41

TORTS CAUSING DEATH

TABLE OF CONTENTS

I. Claims for the Benefit of the Deceased's Dependants

(B) The Statutory Measure of Damages

1. Losses in Respect of which Damages are Not Recoverable or are Recoverable only within Limits

(1) Non-pecuniary loss, except to a spouse, civil partner or parent for bereavement

After para.41-019, add new paragraph:

41-019A   In *Smith v Lancashire Teaching Hospitals NHS Foundation Trust* [2017] EWCA Civ 1916; [2018] Q.B. 804, the Court of Appeal declared that the right to bereavement damages in s.1A of the Fatal Accidents Act was incompatible with art.14 in conjunction with art.8 of the ECHR because, unlike a dependency claim in s.1 of the Act, the claim for bereavement damages excluded cohabitees of two years or more. The claimant, Ms Smith, had co-habited for more than two years with her partner in a relationship that was equivalent to marriage in every respect.

(2) Pecuniary loss by reason of expenses resulting from the death but not related to the pecuniary benefit derived from the continuance of the life, except funeral expenses

(a) Funeral expenses

After the sixth sentence, ending "not always provided.", add:

41-022   Since a reception or wake is not a necessary part of the concept of a funeral those costs should not be recoverable: see also *Blake v Mad Max Ltd* [2018] EWHC 2134 (QB); [2019] P.I.Q.R. Q1 at [17].

2. The Value of the Dependency

(5) Loss of gratuitous services and associated claims

(c) Loss of the intangible cost of arranging for alternative provision of services

To the end of para.41-107, add:

41-107   Unfortunately, this decision was not cited to the Deputy High Court judge in *Blake v Mad Max Ltd* [2018] EWHC 2134 (QB); [2019] P.I.Q.R. Q1 at [42], where he allowed £2,500 for the intangible benefits of a spouse including the time to organise the commercial provision of replacement services.

CHAPTER 42

ASSAULT AND FALSE IMPRISONMENT

TABLE OF CONTENTS

II. FALSE IMPRISONMENT

Add new section at the beginning:

0. DAMAGES AS OF RIGHT

In *R. (on the application of Hemmati) v Secretary of State for the Home Depart-* **42-012A**
ment [2018] EWCA Civ 2122; [2019] Q.B. 708, the question was whether a false
imprisonment that arose due to contravention of EC law needed to be "sufficiently
serious" within the *Factortame* test before damages could be awarded. A majority
of the Court, Sir Terence Etherton MR and Jackson LJ, said at [193] that the
Factortame principle

"has no relevance because the individual right of each human being to liberty exists save
insofar as it is legitimately cut down by law. The right to liberty does not exist because
of the EU and its Charter of Fundamental Rights."

1. HEADS OF DAMAGE

After para.42-013, add a new paragraph:
As we have seen in Ch.17, if detention would have occurred lawfully, but for the **42-013**
false imprisonment, then nominal damages should be awarded unless it can be
shown that the particular detention caused some loss that would not otherwise have
been suffered. Those damages will commonly be nominal. For instance, in *R. (on
the application of Lauzikas) v Secretary of State for the Home Department* [2019]
EWCA Civ 1168, nominal damages were awarded where but for the breach it was
highly likely that detention would have occurred for the same period of time, and
in a lawful manner. An instance where damages might be more than nominal even
if the detention would otherwise have occurred is where it would not have occurred in the same way. Hence, if the breach was significant and had a real effect

on the claimant notwithstanding that he would still have been detained then an award of more than nominal damages can be made. For instance, £250 was awarded for a false imprisonment where detention would have occurred in any event but the unlawful detention arose as a consequence of a failure to respond to serious allegations including torture: *R. (on the application of Le) v Secretary of State for Health and Social Care* [2018] EWHC 3655 (Admin).

To the end of the paragraph, add:

42-015   The smaller award is not made for contributory negligence or failure to mitigate loss but because the harm suffered by, and effect upon, the claimant will generally be less where the claimant is in part the cause of his or her own detention: see *R. (Antonio) v Secretary of State for the Home Department* [2017] EWCA Civ 48; [2017] 1 W.L.R. 3431 at [82]; *R. (on the application of Diop) v Secretary of State for the Home Department* [2018] EWHC 3420 (Admin); [2019] A.C.D. 30 at [74]. Of course, the claimant's conduct must have some "material bearing" on the unlawful detention: *R. (on the application of Diop) v Secretary of State for the Home Department* [2018] EWHC 3420 (Admin); [2019] A.C.D. 30 at [77].

After para.42-017, add a new paragraph:

42-017   In *R. (on the application of Diop) v Secretary of State for the Home Department* [2018] EWHC 3420 (Admin); [2019] A.C.D. 30 the claimant was awarded £9,000 for 28 days of wrongful detention which followed two years of lawful detention. He suffered no initial shock due to the wrongful detention but he became increasingly frustrated when a failure to procure accommodation for him led to delay in his release. In *Majewski v Secretary of State for the Home Department* [2019] EWHC 473 (Admin); [2019] A.C.D. 73, Swift J awarded £14,800 where the initial distress was not out of the ordinary and the claimant had been separated from his wife and children for three years prior to the detention. And in *R. (on the application of KG) v Secretary of State for the Home Department* [2018] EWHC 3665 (Admin), £17,500 plus £2,000 aggravated damages was awarded for 29 days of wrongful detention which followed 24 hours of lawful detention.

Replace para.42-019 with:

42-019   In the most severe group of cases, the period of imprisonment tends to last for months rather than weeks. In *R. (on the application of Belfken) v Secretary of State for the Home Department* [2017] EWHC 1834 (Admin). Ms Karen Steyn QC, sitting as a Deputy High Court judge, made an award of £40,000 for a period of 295 days' unlawful detention without any aggravating factors, or any egregious conduct on the part of the Secretary of State; and in circumstances in which the claimant was, to a degree, uncooperative and obstructive. A shorter period, but with more serious consequences are two claims concerning wrongful detention of the homeless in breach of their EU Treaty rights. In *R. (on the application of Deptka and Sadlowski) v Secretary of State for the Home Department* [2019] EWHC 503 (Admin) the claimants, who were unmarried partners, were wrongfully imprisoned for 154 days. Basic damages of £35,000 were awarded, including £5,000 for the initial shock. They were also awarded aggravated, but not exemplary, damages of £8,500 for the defendant's undue delay in admitting liability and apologising as well as the way the claim was defended, and for the claimants' separation for six weeks, which was particularly distressing for Ms Deptka who was already vulnerable and correspondingly distressing for Mr Sadlowski. Similarly, in *Howlonia v Secretary of State for the Home Department* [2019] EWHC 794 (Admin); [2019] A.C.D. 59, for a false imprisonment of 153 days including lack of medical treatment for a toothache which later led to the need for an operation and high handed treatment of him while he was on a hunger strike, basic damages of £32,000 were awarded, including £6,000 for the initial shock and £5,000, likely as aggravated damages, for the conduct while he was on a hunger strike.

In this group of the most severe cases, where the period of detention is long and there are serious consequences for vulnerable claimants then the award can have a large range. In *AXD v Home Office* [2016] EWHC 1617 (QB) the difference between the award proposed by the applicant and that proposed by the respondent illustrates the great range that still exists in this most severe category of this group of cases. The claimant's false imprisonment was for 614 days and the primary judge, Jay J, awarded £80,000, noting the irrelevance of the allegation that his claim for refugee status should have been recognised sooner and his diagnosis of paranoid schizophrenia (because he was still fit to be detained and a mental health team is readily accessible). His award was modestly increased by fear of being returned to Somalia, and increased because he was kept in his cell for 21 hours a day and he experienced personal difficulties on account of his sexual orientation. In *Mohammed v Home Office* [2017] EWHC 2809 (QB) damages of £78,500 were assessed by Mr Edward Pepperall QC, sitting as a deputy High Court judge, for false imprisonment of a person who, like AXD, had been previously convicted of crimes so that the shock of detention was not as great as a person not previously detained. The period of false imprisonment of 149 days in immigration detention also partly exacerbated his symptoms of post-traumatic stress disorder, and involved culpable conduct of the Home Office including matters that invited "serious criticism" (at [56]). **42-019A**

CHAPTER 43

STATUTORY TORTS: DISCRIMINATION AND HARASSMENT

TABLE OF CONTENTS

I. DISCRIMINATION

1. HEADS OF DAMAGE

(1)   Non-pecuniary loss

Replace para.43-006 with:

As to amounts awarded there was much variety in the earlier days but there is   **43-006**
no longer any need to set out these[9] as in 2002 in *Vento v Chief Constable of West
Yorkshire Police (No.2)*,[10] the Court of Appeal, concerned by a discrimination case
in which an employment tribunal had awarded £100,000 for injury to feelings,[11]
introduced guidelines. The court identified three broad bands for compensation for
injured feelings, a top band of £15,000 to £25,000 for very serious cases, a middle
band of £5,000 to £15,000 for moderately serious cases and a band of £500 to
£5,000 appropriate for less serious cases, such as where the act of discrimination
is an isolated or one-off occurrence. Only in the most exceptional cases, it was said,
would it be appropriate to award more than £25,000, and awards of less than £500
were to be avoided as they risked appearing derisory.[12] In 2009 in *Da'Bell v
National Society for the Prevention of Cruelty to Children*,[13] which involved disability discrimination, the Employment Appeal Tribunal held that the range for
injured feelings damages should be adjusted upwards for inflation as calculated by
the Retail Prices Index, giving a top band from £18,000 to £30,000, a middle band
from £6,000 to £18,000, and the lowest band running up to £6,000.[14] Then, in
September 2017, the President of the Employment Tribunals in England and Wales
and the President of the Employment Tribunals in Scotland issued a guideline (the
Presidential Guidance) called "Employment Tribunal awards for injury to feelings

[113]

and psychiatric injury following *De Souza v Vinci Construction (UK) Ltd* [2017] EWCA Civ 879." The Presidential Guidance provided for an increased in the *Vento* bands from 11 September 2017 as follows: top band of £25,200 to £42,000, middle band of £8,400 to £25,200, and lower band of £800 to £8,400. For claims presented before that date, the Presidential Guidance provides for an inflation formula prior to the application of the *Simmons v Castle* uplift of 10%. However, subsequent cases have followed these guidelines even where the action arose prior to the date of the Guidance: *Durrant v Chief Constable of Avon & Somerset* [2017] EWCA Civ 1808; [2018] I.R.L.R. 263. These Guidelines should last for some time.

⁹ They can be found in the 18th edition of this work.

¹⁰ [2002] EWCA Civ 1871; [2003] I.C.R. 318 CA.

¹¹ Together with aggravated damages of £25,000; see [2002] EWCA Civ 1871; [2003] I.C.R. 318 CA at [46] and [47].

¹² The Employment Tribunal in *Vento* had awarded £50,000 for injury to feelings, reduced by the Employment Appeal Tribunal and further reduced by the Court of Appeal to £18,000.

¹³ [2010] I.R.L.R. 19.

¹⁴ [2010] I.R.L.R. 19 at [44].

Replace para.43-007 with:

43-007   The three bands, as updated, have stood the test of time and the courts continue to pay attention to them. For purposes of comparison, however, the most useful cases are likely to be those that postdate the relevant Guidelines, here the most recent being September 2017. One of the earliest examples of application of the 2017 Guidelines is *Durrant v Chief Constable of Avon & Somerset* [2017] EWCA Civ 1808; [2018] I.R.L.R. 263. In that case, the police engaged in racially discriminatory conduct, by subconscious bias, when they had (i) focused upon arresting the appellant, (ii) handcuffed her hands behind her back causing her to be thrown around in the back of the police van and (unknown to her) being laughed at by the police, and (iii) delayed for a significant time in allowing the appellant to go to the toilet at the police station, causing the appellant to urinate on the floor of the holding cell in front of a group of male officers. Applying the *Vento* guidelines (*Vento v Chief Constable of West Yorkshire Police (No.2)* [2002] EWCA Civ 1871; [2003] I.C.R. 318 CA), the case was found to fall within the lower part of the middle band. An award of £14,000 was made taking into account all of the circumstances, and following the 2017 Presidential Guidance because, even though the claim was brought before the 2017 Presidential Guidance, this was thought to be the simplest way to take inflation into account. The unconscious nature of the discrimination, although it had humiliating consequences, made it inappropriate for an award of aggravated or exemplary damages.

II.   HARASSMENT

1.   HEADS OF DAMAGE

(1)   Non-pecuniary loss

To the end of para.43-019, add:

43-019   Again, in *Suttle v Walker* [2019] EWHC 396 (QB) an award of £40,000 in general damages, which appears vastly beyond the usual range, is explicable because the judge, Nicklin J, included within the award amounts for injury to reputation (as part of a defamation claim) as well as an amount for the seriousness of the harassment.

CHAPTER 46

DEFAMATION

TABLE OF CONTENTS

Replace para.46-001 with:

The tort of defamation, looked at from the point of view of damages, has histori- **46-001**
cally been broken into two parts. On the one hand there were defamatory statements actionable only on proof of special damage, with a special meaning attach-
ing in this connection to the term special damage; on the other hand there were
defamatory statements actionable per se. The first category comprises most slanders,
and the second the remaining slanders and all libels. It remains useful to treat these
categories separately although the distinction between them has been much reduced
by additional requirement in s.1 of the Defamation Act 2013 that a statement is not
defamatory unless "in fact" (*Lachaux v Independent Print Ltd* [2019] UKSC 27;

[2019] 3 W.L.R. 18 at [11]) it had caused or was likely to cause serious harm to the claimant's reputation.

46-001A　　Section 1 of the Defamation Act 2013 makes the causing "serious harm to the reputation", a pre-condition of recovery for defamation. Where the body said to be defamed is a body that trades for profit then s.1(2) requires that serious financial loss must be suffered. In *Lachaux*, the Supreme Court held that the requirement of "serious harm" and, in the case of bodies trading for profit, "serious financial harm" is not the same as the requirement for special damage. The serious harm, and serious financial harm, must arise from injury to reputation. But special damage can arise from any other loss that is caused by the defamatory remark, irrespective of whether the loss is concerned with an interest other than reputation. In that case, serious harm was actually suffered as a result of the publication of articles that falsely accused the claimant including of being violent and abusive towards his wife and acting to deprive her of custody of their son including falsely accusing her of abduction.

II.　Slanders Actionable Per Se and Libel

2.　Heads of Damage

(1)　Injury to reputation

After the second paragraph, add a new paragraph:

46-031　　The usual assessment of injury to reputation will require consideration of (i) the claimant's role in society and the relation of the defamatory statements upon that role; (ii) the identity of the publisher of the statement with the associated authority and credibility afforded to the statement; and (iii) the identity of the persons to whom the statement is published and the associated effect of the statement which may be less likely to be believed by those who know the claimant well but could be likely to last longer; and, although more relevant to the vindication element of damages, (iv) the propensity of the statement to "percolate through underground channels and contaminate hidden springs" (*Suttle v Walker* [2019] EWHC 396 (QB) at [21]).

(3)　The references to vindication

After para.46-035, add a new paragraph:

46-035A　　With the focus of the award upon amelioration of any future adverse consequences, either pecuniary or non-pecuniary, the size of the award under this head will therefore depend on factors such as (i) the seriousness of the allegation, its likely "sticking power" and the "grapevine effect", (ii) future publicity including media reports of the trial and judgment, and (iii) any apology made by the defendant and the extent of the publicity or dissemination of the apology: *Dhir v Saddler* [2017] EWHC 3155 (QB); [2018] 4 W.L.R. 1 at [103], [108], [110].

To the end of para.40-036, add:

46-036　　In *Dhir v Saddler* and *Monir v Wood* [2018] EWHC 3525 (QB), in each of which there were a number of matters of mitigation, Nickin J awarded £35,000 and £40,000 respectively for words spoken by the defendant at a church meeting, saying that the claimant had threatened to "slit my throat" and for a Tweet that described the claimant as a "suspended child grooming taxi driver" from an account with limited followers where very limited recipients other than his neighbour and people in the local area would have understood that it referred to the claimant. In contrast, in *Suttle v Walker* [2019] EWHC 396 (QB), where the award of damages for the head of injury to reputation took into account the extent of the grapevine or percolation effect (see at [48]), Nicklin J concluded that there did not need to be much, if any, "uplift in this figure for the purposes of vindication" (at [59]).

CHAPTER 47

INVASION OF PRIVACY

1. HEADS OF DAMAGE

(1) Non-pecuniary loss

After para.47-008, add a new paragraph:

By far the largest award for breach of privacy was made in *Richard v The Brit-* **47-008A**
ish Broadcasting Corp [2018] EWHC 1837 (Ch); [2019] Ch. 169. That case
involved a finding by Mann J that the BBC had infringed the privacy rights of Sir
Cliff Richard, a 73 year old entertainer, by publication of details of an investiga-
tion into allegations of a historic sexual offence for which he was not ultimately
charged. The infringement, and consequently the size of the general damages, was
considered to be much more serious than that in Mosley in light of the allegations
involved, the nationwide instant transmission to many people by a national
broadcaster several times in a day, the republication and enormous publicity, the
triggering of publications by others, and the profound effect that publication had
on Sir Cliff (at [349]). The award of £190,000 in general damages was based upon
all of the related matters and consequences including distress and damage to health
(at [350(a)]. In addition, other factors that increased the damages, which apparently included elements independent of any distress suffered, were for the "deprivation of his right to control the use of his private information", and damage to his
"dignity, status and reputation". Mann J rejected the submission that general damages for infringement of privacy could not include a component for damage to
reputation. Defamation is not the sole province for the protection of reputation, it
can be protected also by the tort of infringement of privacy: *Khuja v Times
Newspapers Ltd* [2017] UKSC 49; [2019] A.C. 161 at [21], [34], [381]. Of course,
there should not be double recovery for injury to reputation if the interest is violated
by both defamation and infringement of privacy. Many of these factors represented
a broad range of possible but unquantifiable consequences including the general
adverse effect on Sir Cliff's lifestyle (at [350(b)]), future distress and other future
consequences. One future consequence which materialised, and which led to an
award of an additional $20,000 aggravated damages, was the BBC submitting its
broadcast for an award, although it did not win the award. That conduct showed a

lack of repentance and it repeated the infringement with "metaphorical fanfare" (at [365]).

To the end of the paragraph, add:

47-009   And in *Ali v Channel 5 Broadcasting Ltd* [2019] EWCA Civ 677, the claimants obtained damages of £10,000 for unjustified infringement of their privacy rights by a television programme that portrayed footage of their eviction from their rental home. On an appeal based on inadequacy of damages, the Court of Appeal upheld an award of £10,000, concluding that it was not so low as "to be perverse" (at [119]). One factor in the reduction of damages was that a number of people in the claimants' community were already aware of the events during the eviction because social media postings of the event by the landlord and his son.

(2)   "Right to control information": restitutionary damages for the opportunity taken

Replace para.47-011 with:

47-011   The award for the claimant's "lost right to control private information" should be understood as an instance of the unconventional award for loss commonly described as "user damages". In *Gulati v MGN Ltd* the Court of Appeal, rightly, insisted that the award was not given to "vindicate" the right to control the information. The Court of Appeal also accepted that this award was not for any other non-financial consequence actually experienced by the claimant (including distress). The basis for the award is best understood as the value of the opportunity to use information without paying for that opportunity. As Mann J, at first instance, said (*Gulati v MGN Ltd* [2015] EWHC 1482 (Ch); [2016] F.S.R. 12 at [132]):

> "the defendant will have helped itself, over an extended period of time, to large amounts of personal and private information and treated it as its own to deal with as it thought fit".

It is elementary justice that the defendant should have to pay the reasonable price for that opportunity or benefit, in addition to an award for the distress to the claimant. As explained in Ch.14 understanding the nature of the award will also aid the court in quantifying how the damages can be calculated such as, in circumstances which the Court of Appeal in *Gulati v MGN Ltd* rightly accepted that the amount awarded would be affected, if the information had become public knowledge anyway: See also *Burrell v Clifford* [2016] EWHC 294 (Ch); [2017] E.M.L.R. 2 at [45].

Replace para.47-012 with:

47-012   The focus on the value of the opportunity to control information has the benefit of transparently valuing this head of damages rather than the approach, sometimes adopted by counsel and reflected in decisions such as *TLT v Secretary of State for the Home Department* [2016] EWHC 2217 (QB); [2016] Info. T.L.R. 373, where the damages are awarded as a single amount without a separate award in respect of this head of damage.

47-012A   This characterisation of the right to control information as a type of "user damages" was not accepted by Warby J in *Lloyd v Google LLC* [2018] EWHC 2599 (QB); [2019] 1 W.L.R. 1265. The nature of damages for an infringement of privacy arose in that case in the context of an application for permission to serve proceedings on Google LLC, a foreign corporation. The proceedings alleged a breach by

Google of s.4(4) of the Data Protection Act 1998 by secretly tracking, collating, using, and selling data concerning the internet activity of Apple iPhone users. The claimant sued on his own behalf and on behalf of a class of other English residents for damage suffered under s.13 of the Act. One reason that Warby J refused leave to serve out because the statutory requirement for "damage" suffered in the jurisdiction had not been satisfied. The simplest answer to the claim would have been that damage under s.13 of the Act requires loss in the conventional sense and does not include user (or negotiating)) damages: see *Murray v Express Newspapers Plc* [2007] EWHC 1908 (Ch); [2007] E.M.L.R. 22. It should have been enough to say that, following *Murray v Express Newspapers*, the claim should fail because it was not alleged that any financial loss had been suffered or that distress had resulted: *Lloyd v Google LLC* [2018] EWHC 2599 (QB); [2019] 1 W.L.R. 1265 at [3]. As Warby J observed, mere "loss of control" over personal data establishes an infringement but does not establish loss or damage in the conventional sense; some people are "quite happy" to have their personal information collected in order to receive advertising or marketing (at [58]–[59], [74]). However, Warby J went further and held that the award in *Gulati* was separate and distinct from a user damages award (at [81]). He held that it was, although accepting that *Gulati* had not sanctioned the award of damages for the mere fact of misuse of personal information (at [70]). But it is hard to see what other basis there could be for the loss of control over personal information other than as "user" or "negotiating" damages. Indeed, an example given by Lord Reed in *Morris-Garner v One Step (Support) Ltd* [2018] UKSC 20; [2019] A.C. 649 of his conceptualisation of user damages as "an unconventional loss" was where confidential information is misused resulting in the loss of "a valuable opportunity to exercise their right to control the use of the information" (*Morris-Garner* at [84]). That unconventional loss arises from the owner being prevented from "exercising his right to obtain the economic value of the use in question" (*Morris-Garner* at [30]).

(3)   Pecuniary loss

After para.47-014, add a new paragraph:
    The most significant examples of pecuniary loss arising from a breach of privacy **47-014A** can be seen in the decision of Mann J in *Richard v The British Broadcasting Corp* [2018] EWHC 1837 (Ch); [2019] Ch. 169. Although Mann J was not asked to quantify any of the pecuniary loss, the parties sought and obtained findings on issues of causation. Mann J held that several events of loss were caused by the BBC's contravention of Sir Cliff's privacy rights. These were: the legal costs to have Facebook take down a hostile group that was formed on the same day as the BBC's publicity surrounding the search of Sir Cliff's premises; the legal costs of preventing or correcting proposed publications in print and broadcast media that would not have occurred within the BBC's publication; responding to blackmail threats; and a lost book advance.

2.   AGGRAVATION AND MITIGATION

After para.47-015, add a new paragraph:
    Aggravated damages of $20,000 for infringement of privacy were awarded in **47-015A** *Richard v The British Broadcasting Corp* [2018] EWHC 1837 (Ch); [2019] Ch. 169 when the BBC submitted its contravening broadcast concerning Sir Cliff Richard for an award. By doing so it showed a lack of repentance and repeated the infringe-

ment of privacy with "metaphorical fanfare" (at [365]). However, other factors did not lead to further aggravated damages: the disregard for his rights was not flagrant (in the sense of reckless) (at [363]); the refusal to admit liability was not out of the ordinary (at [364]); and the BBC's defence of the action was not out of the ordinary (at [366]–[367]).

CHAPTER 48

ECONOMIC TORTS AND INTELLECTUAL PROPERTY WRONGS

TABLE OF CONTENTS

V. INFRINGEMENT OF RIGHTS IN INTELLECTUAL PROPERTY

2. THE PRESENT ENGLISH LAW, THE DIRECTIVE APART

(ii) Relation with exemplary damages

After para.48-065, add a new paragraph:

This vexed question of the nature of additional damages was finally put to rest **48-065A** in a magisterial judgment of Lewison LJ, with whom Eleanor King LJ and David Richards LJ agreed, in *Phonographic Performance Ltd v Ellis (t/a Bla Bla Bar)* [2018] EWCA Civ 2812; [2019] Bus. L.R. 542. The issue in that case concerned whether additional damages should be awarded when a suspended sentence of imprisonment had also been awarded for contempt in breaching an injunction to restrain the copyright infringement. Lewison LJ referred to the point of principle discussed in the paragraph above (at [33]) and powerfully observed that in 1977, after *Rookes v Barnard* [1964] A.C. 1129; [1964] 2 W.L.R. 269, the Whitford Committee had reported on copyright law and treated additional damages as encompassing exemplary damages awards (at [24]–[26]). The substantive change to s.97(2) of the Copyright Designs and Patents Act 1988 that was made following the report of the Whitford Committee, which would be redundant unless additional damages extended to exemplary damages, was to remove the restriction on the award of additional damages that restricted them to cases in which relief, effective to compensate, would not otherwise be available to the claimant (at [34]–[36]). Ultimately, Lewison LJ concluded that the trial judge had erred in concluding that additional damages, like a criminal sentence or fine, precluded an exemplary award, when neither did so (at [57]). Nevertheless, and notwithstanding the suspended criminal sentence, the circumstances of breach in the case did not establish the flagrancy sufficient for an award of additional damages.

(iii)   Criteria for assessment

To the end of the paragraph, add:

48-068   And in *Reformation Publishing Co Ltd v Cruiseco Ltd* [2018] EWHC 2761 (Ch); [2019] Bus. L.R. 78, Nugee J awarded £25,000 by way of additional damages for the recklessness of the defendant's agent amounting to flagrancy. The trial judge was cited no authority and was provided with few submissions as to quantum but, given the finding of recklessness "at the lowest" (at [87]), his award of £25,000 additional damages on top of £38,750 damages was aligned with the award in less flagrant circumstances in *Nottingham Healthcare NHS Trust v News Group Newspapers Ltd* [2002] EWHC 409 (Ch); [2002] R.P.C. 49 of almost £10,000 additional damages with £450 damages.

3.   THE IMPACT OF THE EUROPEAN DIRECTIVE

(2)   Application by the courts

Replace the paragraph with:

48-077   In the light of all this, how have the English courts seen and applied these new requirements stemming from Europe? What is interesting is that scant attention has been paid in the English cases to these provisions. Although they have been in force since April 2006, just two cases are known in which they have been invoked and relied upon. The one, dealing with the infringement of the claimant companies' right in the performance and recording of a concert, was heard in 2010 in the High Court; this was *Experience Hendrix LLC v Times Newspapers Ltd*.[429] The other, dealing with the infringement of the claimant company's patent, was heard in 2013 in the Patent County Court; this was *Xena Systems Ltd v Cantideck*.[430] There is the thought, which should perhaps not be expressed, that counsel and court were unaware of this exceptional intrusion of the European Union into the English law of damages. The more likely explanation is that the position under the Directive article and the United Kingdom regulation is seen as being no different from the position at common law, so that there was no need to turn to them.[431] Certainly, Sir William Blackburne in his judgment in the *Experience Hendrix* case, moved easily between Directive and English authorities which suggests that he was of much the same view, awarding loss of profits from a perfectly English law standpoint[432] and making no increase in the damages on account of moral prejudice.[433] As for *Xena v Cantideck* Judge Birss's full judgment is almost entirely taken up with working out the claimant company's loss of profits with reliance solely on English authorities, has little reference to the Directive article and briefly refuses to award any damages for moral prejudice.[434] A third, *Phonographic Performance Ltd v Ellis (t/a Bla Bla Bar)* [2018] EWCA Civ 2812; [2019] Bus. L.R. 542, held after careful consideration that an award of additional damages, in the nature of an exemplary award, was more favourable to the right-holder and not likely to be affected by the Directive (at [40]). The only possible exception to this might be if the award is so excessive that it could amount to an abuse of rights (at [42]). However, fourthly, and finally, in *Ghias v Grill'O Xpress Ltd* [2018] EWHC 3445 (IPEC) at [51] it was suggested, following *Henderson v All Around the World Recordings Ltd* [2014] EWHC 3087 (IPEC) at [80], that art.13(1)(a) contemplated an additional award of damages where the four heads described above were not adequate to compensate the claimant then there is "flexibility" to award an additional sum related to the profit that the defendant has made from the knowing infringement. This looks remarkably like additional damages but shorn from any ability to make an exemplary award. Again, English law would continue to apply.

[429] [2010] EWHC 1986 (Ch).

[430] [2013] EWPCC 1; [2013] F.S.R. 41.

[431] The Directive indeed requires an application by the injured party for its provisions on damages to be brought in; there is no equivalent in the UK's wording. Compare art.13.1 with reg.3(1), both at para.48-038, above.

[432] See details of the case at para.10-004, above.

[433] [2010] EWHC 1986 (Ch) at [73]–[76].

[434] [2013] EWPCC 1; [2013] F.S.R. 41 at [114].

MISREPRESENTATION

I.   FRAUDULENT MISREPRESENTATION: DECEIT

2.   HEADS OF DAMAGE

(1)   Pecuniary loss

(c)   Where the contract is other than for shares

(i)   Normal measure

After para.49-028, add a new paragraph:

In exceptional cases, however, the value received by the claimant's entry into a **49-028A** contract with a third party will be disregarded. In *Barker v Winter* [2018] EWHC 1785 (QB), the claimant was deceived by the defendant into believing that he was a man of considerable wealth. In reliance upon his fraudulent misrepresentations, she spent hundreds of thousands of pounds on a "lavish lifestyle" including expenditure on expensive foreign travel, hotels, restaurants, cars, clothes and gifts. Judge Rawlings held that these benefits did not have a sufficient degree of permanence to be taken into account when calculating the loss suffered (at [28]). It may be that although the claimant would not otherwise have spent the money on the lavish lifestyle, some allowance could have been taken to reflect the enjoyment that she derived. It is likely that, objectively, the lifestyle that she enjoyed would have had some pecuniary value to a person in her position even if the money would not have been spent at the full price. But the value of a credit for benefits received is for a defendant to prove: *Parallel Imports (Europe) Ltd v Radivan* [2007] EWCA Civ 1373 at [34]–[35].

(ii) Consequential losses

Replace para.49-032 with:

49-032   In *Dadourian Group International Inc v Simms*,[150] the claimant was a seller rather than a buyer. The defendant's deceit having caused the claimant to contract to sell hospital bed manufacturing equipment to a third party, the claimant sought to claim loss of profits from being deprived of entering into an alternative sale agreement with another purchaser. Dealing with the issue of damages at the end of a very long judgment,[151] Warren J without any reference to *East v Maurer* considered this to be a good head of claim, but was not prepared to admit it as he had neither evidence that an alternative sale would have been available[152] nor evidence of the value that an alternative sale would have commanded.[153] The case went to the Court of Appeal[154] but there was no appeal by the claimant on this adverse holding,[155] the appeal being on another issue on damages.[156] An *East v Maurer* claim by a seller was successful in *Khakshouri v Jiminez* [2017] EWHC 3392 (QB), where the loss suffered arose from the loss of an opportunity to invest funds that had been diverted to a loan. The loan had been induced by the deceit of the defendants. The defendants repaid the loan. It later turned out that the investment would have been very profitable for the claimant. The defendants submitted that any loss should be assessed at the date of repayment, when the investment was not known to be profitable. The claimant alleged that the loss should be assessed at a later date when he would have realised the profit on the investment that he would have made, but for the deceit. The judge held that the usual rule did not apply and the date of assessment was not the date that the funds were repaid. Just as the usual rule does not apply where a claimant is locked into a transaction, it did not apply here where the claimant had been locked "out" of the investment for which the funds would otherwise have been used (at [180]).

[150] [2006] EWHC 2973 (Ch). See also *Inter Export LLC v Townley* [2017] EWHC 530 (Ch) at [8].

[151] [2006] EWHC 2973 (Ch) at [747] and following.

[152] [2006] EWHC 2973 (Ch) at [755].

[153] [2006] EWHC 2973 (Ch) at [756]. He also held that the claimant's decision to scrap the equipment was a clear failure to mitigate: at [754].

[154] [2009] EWCA Civ 169; [2009] 1 Lloyd's Rep. 601 CA.

[155] This comes out at [2009] EWCA Civ 169 at [117].

[156] See para.49-035, below.

Replace footnote 173 with:

49-035   [173] See at [109]–[148], affirming Warren J at [2006] EWHC 2973 (Ch) at [758]–[761] and at [2007] EWHC 454 (Ch) at [22]–[24]. In *Khakshouri v Jiminez* [2017] EWHC 3392 (QB) the claimant was also held to have mitigated the loss.

(d)   Where there is no contract

After para.49-039, add a new paragraph:

49-039A   The result in *Smith Kline* has been questioned because of this departure from the compensatory principle. In *Smith New Court Securities v Scrimgeour Vickers* [1997] A.C. 254 at 283, Lord Steyn referred to the view of Professor Burrows that *Smith Kline* had been incorrectly decided but Lord Steyn did not need to decide the point.

In *Inter Export LLC v Townley* [2018] EWCA Civ 2068, Arden LJ (with whom Birss J and Kitchin LJ agreed) accepted that the decision in *Smith Kline* was binding on the Court of Appeal and suggested that it might be explained by a special rule for the measurement of loss for deceit (at [66]). It may be that the "special rule", like that for conversion, and like that for the award of negotiating damages, represents the value of the impairment of the claimant's rights, which are themselves an asset, irrespective of ultimate financial loss. But the point did not need to be decided in the *Inter Export LLC* case. There, representations as to creditworthiness were continuing representations and were relied upon with the effect that the claimant lost title to sunflower oil that it had purchased from a third party.

(2)   Non-pecuniary loss

(c)   Mental distress

Replace para.49-045 with:

In *Archer v Brown*,[223] Pain J had relied on the analogy from contract, but this is **49-045** a somewhat empty, dangerous analogy which, though in the past it may have hindered the acceptance of damages for mental distress in deceit, can now only help, in the changed contractual climate[224]; he could see no reason in logic or justice why damages for injured feelings should not be awarded in deceit on the same basis as in contract.[225] However, Pain J's reference to these damages as aggravated damages,[226] a reference which has found its way into the headnote, is not entirely accurate. The true position is that a claimant should be entitled to compensation for any mental distress he has suffered; such damages will become aggravated damages only if they fall to be increased because the heinousness of the defendant's conduct is considered to have added to the claimant's suffering.[227] The same unfortunate conflation occurred in *Barker v Winter* [2018] EWHC 1785 (QB) at [67], with the result that despite the judge accepting that considerable distress was suffered, no damages were awarded because they could not be brought within aggravated damages. The decision on this point might better be understood as a denial of mental distress damages where there had been a failure to bring into account, in assessing the other heads of damages claimed, the compensating benefit of a lavish lifestyle arising from the money spent by the claimant (see above at para.49-028A). As for *A v B*,[228] the analogy from bereavement in fatal injury cases was presented by counsel to Sir John Blofeld, but he considered that, although the claimant's distress was very real, it could not be as severe as a bereavement which is final and irreversible.[229] Yet surely the paternity of the child was equally final and irreversible.

[223] [1985] Q.B. 401; [1984] 3 W.L.R. 350.

[224] See paras 5-024 and following, above.

[225] [1985] Q.B. 401 at 426F.

[226] See [1985] Q.B. 401 at 402G, and 414E together with 424B and 426D.

[227] Compare the more developed position with defamation at paras 46-031 and following, and paras 46-043 and following, above.

[228] [2007] EWHC 1246 (QB); [2007] 2 F.L.R. 1051.

[229] [2007] EWHC 1246 (QB); [[2007] 2 F.L.R. 1051 at [57].